This book is dedicated to the teachings of "Lord Krishna"
And
Blessings of my parents.

Special thanks to the light of my life, my wife Alka Sharma who always stood by me; and my son Parth Sharma who constantly motivated me to see the positive side of the coin.

One more person who needs to be acknowledged is my brother Anurag Sharma, who always kept reminding me that I need to finish what I have started.

Disclaimer

The Character and events portrayed in this book are fictitious. Any similarity to real persons, living or dead, or actual events or names, characters, businesses, places, events and incidents are purely coincidental and not intended by the author.

Table of Contents

Chapter-1

(The Arrival of Guest)

It was a fine sunny day. The bright sunshine, gentle breeze, dark clouds at horizon; together they were making the appearance picturesque.

The chirping of birds was being complimented by the cheers of teens. Every one around was happy and relaxed, so was I; sitting lazily under the shade of a banyan tree.

Nature possesses the ability to refresh mind and comfort the soul; a refreshed mind always thinks better. So, whenever I have got a little time with me or I am unhappy or stressed out, I always come to this park in search of peace and comfort.

I truly like it here but my overburdened schedule doesn't allow me to visit this place frequently. Today, I am here because I am a little confused and not able to think straight.

I always had my share of sorrows and hard times before but I have never felt this shallow and clueless in my life.

I am a hardworking person having the roll up your sleeves attitude. Understandably, I have achieved a lot in my life. A good job, a corner office, luxury life style and a lot of recognition and appreciation, I have got all the fame and money that one can desire and that too at a very young age.

In a way, it won't be wrong to say that I have a life worth envying.

In fact, I am due for my next big and most awaited promotion in the office. Even after so much good happening around me, I don't know why, but still I am not happy with myself?

Unfortunately, even this most awaited promotion has also failed to kindle the spark of happiness inside me. It feels like, as if, I want something badly in my life but don't know what exactly it is and where to look for it.

Don't misjudge me to be a depressed or a lonely person. It's nothing like that but my inability to find the reason behind this feeling of emptiness has further worsened the situation.

This process of introspection was interrupted by few loud voices. I gazed around with curiosity and noticed a person arguing with a group of teenagers. The more he scolded them louder grew their laughter, which was further infuriating the already agitated old man.

He might be having some valid reasons behind his anger but still he reminded me of my college friend who was just like him; a troublemaker and a real time show spoiler.

No matter what the situation was; he possessed an in diminishing potential to spoil the event. Either he himself was into the trouble or he would drag others into one. His wicked smile was not only scary but was the indicator of impending doom.

I decided not to spoil my weekend by revisiting those memories from past, so I focused on the playground. I was enjoying the moment and was laughing at the mischievousness of the young kids. Eventually, it was turning out be a pleasant day.

A sudden pat on my shoulder interrupted this state of euphoria, and the pat was followed by a voice, "Is it you? What a pleasant surprise! How are you?

(I turned around and to my surprise he was the very same person I had just thought about. I cursed myself for remembering him. I was shocked at the promptness with which god converted my thoughts into reality.)

With a false enthusiasm and fake smile I greeted him and said, "Hey buddy, how are you? It is good to see you. Look at you; you haven't changed a bit."

He was accompanied by a well dressed old man. I could sense his uneasiness as my friend forgot to introduce him. So, I asked while looking inquiringly towards the old man, "Who is this gentleman standing besides you?

Realizing his mistake he said apologizing, "Oh! I forgot to introduce him. He is my uncle, a professor of human psychology and is here to do some research work in the university."

(I greeted him politely. I always have an inclination towards elderly and educated people, as one can learn a lot from them. After conversing a little with him, I came to know that he was indeed a knowledgeable person having excellent oratory skills. In a very short duration, I developed an acquaintance with him).

I was surprised to see that this time my friend was behaving very differently, he was looking happy and was nowhere even near to the troubles.

I said while placing my hand on his shoulder, "You have changed a lot".

"I don't think so" He replied instantly.

His reply confused me a little; however, before I could utter a word, he asked me, "Do you still live in that big house?"

"Yes I do and now I have expanded a little" I replied with pride as we walked towards a nearby bench.

I continued and said out of courtesy, "You should visit sometime".

(It was clear from my statement that I was not directly inviting him to my home and I had expected him to reply accordingly. I mean he could have said, surely I will visit sometime or sure will give you a call when I am in the town next time. But what he said was absolutely unexpected.)

In response to my offer he smiled and continued walking towards the bench.

I could sense the trouble just by looking at his wicked smile.

He gave a quick glance towards his uncle and said while placing his left hand on my shoulder, "This is excellent; I think you would not mind if my uncle stays with you for about a month or so. Actually, I am going out on a business trip and was looking for a suitable accommodation to lodge him."

(I was speechless on hearing to his proposal. I mean, who goes out on a month long business trip and why can't he find even a single suitable accommodation in such a big city.)

Without caring for my response he continued and said while sitting on the adjacent bench, "After a long tiring search, we had come to this park to catch some breath. Here we found you. You have always helped me in past, I hope you are also going to help me today, aren't you?"

(When he was bombarding me with his intentions, I thought to myself, "He was right about himself, he has not changed even a bit. He was the trouble maker then and still he is one". I wish, I hadn't come to this park today and even if I came, then I shouldn't have thought about him.)

Before I could give any response to him, he asked again, "Are you not going to help me?"

"Of course, I am definitely going to help the professor." I replied with fake enthusiasm.

I looked towards the professor and said while taking out my visiting card from my pocket, "Professor here is my visiting card you can drop in whenever you like and can stay as long as you wish to".

Professor took it from me and thanked me for the much needed help.

Before leaving they thanked me again and we shook our hands. Although, I wanted to grab my friend by his neck but this time I had to suffice with his hand only.

After they left, the bright sunshine transformed into scorching sunrays, birds chirping and children laughter became noises and clouds started looking ugly and threatening with thunder.

That day, I realized that things change with our perspective. Perhaps, that's why it is very difficult to sustain relations in a healthy state as our emotions and feelings often keeps on changing with our perspectives, so does our behavior.

With a sad heart and heavy feet I paved my way back to my house while constantly thinking that, "I should not have visited this park today".

Soon I was at my home waiting for the devil to knock at my doorsteps. Although accommodating someone in not a big deal but a little uneasiness on my behalf was justified. As it was an absolute invasion of my personal space and that too without any warning, forget about my consent.

As sun was about to set, a car came speeding towards my house, there was nothing much left to guess. I already knew the occupants. Here goes the doorbell. My servant opened the door and guided them to the terrace where I was standing and trying to drown my anger with the setting sun.

I greeted them and offered tea and snacks to them. After chatting for a while we had our dinner. My friend left after dinner and now it was the professor and I left to tide over.

The professor took a complete tour of my mansion and genuinely appreciated the entire house. However, what he liked most about the house was my study.

Although, he was not the first one to appreciate the study, as it often manages to catch eyeballs owing to its peaceful and comforting ambience and a very wide front window offering a tranquil view of the forest.

Everything in study is arranged in such a manner that sitting in here feels like as if you are sitting in the nature's lap.

Apart from the vibes of the study, he also appreciated the collection of books that I had stocked up in there.

He placed his hands on the backrest of the study chair and said thoughtfully, "Would you mind, if I may use your study to work on my project. It's quite comforting and free from distractions."

"Please, you may. Moreover, I seldom get a chance to sit in here." I replied promptly as I walked towards the study table.

I picked up few of my belongings that were lying scattered on the table and said, "Jerry will clean this table for you. If you need anything else please feel free to ask him. He will be happy to help you."

 "Thanks for your generosity. I really appreciate it." Professor replied while walking towards the sofa.

(The best way to know about a person is to talk to him. So I decided to start a little conversation with him.)

I placed my stuff on an empty rack near the bookshelves, walked towards the sofa where the professor was sitting and said while sitting on the sofa chair placed across him, "Sir, if you do not mind can I ask you something?"

"Please go ahead." He replied as he put down the magazine that he had just picked up and was about to open it to read.

I asked, "Sir, what do you teach and what brings you here?"

"I teach human psychology and philosophy, and also work as a motivator. I am here to do research for my new book." He replied.

I said, "Well this sounds interesting and cumbersome too"

He laughed a little and asked, "What do you do young man? You own a very big house."

"Sir, my work is not as interesting as yours. I am an Asstt. VP with a software firm and this is my ancestral home. I have made few additions to it." I replied humbly.

Professor said in an affirming tone, "Assistant Vice President at this age, quite impressive. Well I must say you do look like one, well behaved, well dressed and kempt. A person demeanor tells a lot about him"

He continued as he shifted a little while sitting on sofa, "I have seen many people whose appearance and behavior is just not reflective of the chair they hold."

"Thanks for appreciating me. However, I must say you are also not as boring and bland as I had expected you to be." I replied candidly.

He laughed a little and said smilingly, "I think we are going to have a great time ahead"

I nodded in acceptance and smiled back at him.

After that we had an informative and enriching discussion on various other topics. I was right to not stereotype him. He was a great man with a legit knowledge of various subjects.

It won't be wrong to consider him as a well learned, experienced and knowledgeable person.

While having conversation I glanced at my watch and was surprised to know that it was already half past 11 pm. I don't remember the last time when I had such an informative and engaging conversation with anyone.

I said while pointing towards the watch, "It was a very engrossing conversation, I must have lost the track of time.

I continued as I called Jerry. "You must be tired so I won't keep you awake any longer"

"That's all right; I have got all of the night with me to get some rest." Professor replied while getting up from the sofa.

Jerry has already prepared bed for the professor. We wished good night to each other and walked to our respective rooms.

....✳ ✳ ✳..

Chapter – 2

(How to Make Time & the Concept of Time Log Sheet)

"A time spent wisely is the best investment a person can make in his life"

I Meekly opened my eyes and tried to glance at the table clock. Suddenly my eyes got opened wide, when I realized that it was already 7 in the morning; which implied that I was running late for almost everything, including my meeting with the clients.

I rushed my way to the washroom and by 7:30am I was all dressed up. While walking towards the dining room, I hurriedly stuffed my files into the office bag.

Professor was already sitting at dining table and jerry was serving him with breakfast. As I entered the dining room, Jerry wished me and said (as he paced his way towards the gas stove), "Good morning sir, please take a seat. Let me serve you with your breakfast."

"Make is fast, I am running late" I said as I placed the office bag on sofa and walked towards the dining table.

I greeted the professor as I pulled out a chair for me.

He smiled and said after gulping down the coffee he had already sipped, "Good morning dear, you look so stressed out. Don't you think that it's a little early to feel so?"

I smiled and said before gobbling down my sandwich, "I can't help it. It's my morning drill. Don't worry; over a period of time, you will get to know me better."

"Sure, looking forward to it" Professor replied and asked the jerry for a refill.

I asked him after finishing my food, "You look so tidied up, are you going somewhere? I can drop you."

"I am going to the National University; there I am supposed to attend a meeting with the faculty members. Don't worry, I will manage. But thanks for asking," replied professor.

I said while getting up from the table, "Oh come on professor, I can easily drop you there. The university you intend to visit is en-route to my office. It won't be a problem."

I said as I picked up my office bag from the sofa, "Let's go now".

Professor got up from the dining table, thanked Jerry for a lovely meal and headed straight towards the door. Meanwhile, I quickly paced my way towards the porch to unlock the car. Thankfully, I had parked the car in the porch, had it been in the garage it would have surely delayed me by at least 5 minutes time.

Professor quickly hopped inside the car and without wasting a moment we started with our journey.

As we drove out of the gate I asked him after merging on the highway, "Sir, when is your meeting scheduled?"

"At 9:00 am" professor replied calmly.

I glanced at my watch it was 8:30 am. I said admiringly, "Spot on, you would be there on time, in fact a little earlier."

I glanced into the rearview mirror, before changing the lane and said while merging in, "I don't know why but I am almost late for everything. In a sense, I am always in a state of hurry."

I said candidly, "Sometimes I wish that the day should have at least 26 or may be 27 hours instead of 24, so that everyone will be able to meet the deadlines without any burn out."

"I think 24-hours in a day are more than enough. In case you are finding them insufficient then you should learn to make time" Professor replied thoughtfully.

Listening to his reply, I glanced a little at him surprisingly and said while looking back on the road, "Professor, till today I have heard about time management but have never heard about this. How can anyone make time for himself?"

"It is quite possible and I am doing this for years. That's why I have never missed on any deadline or been late to anything, at least not since the last decade." He replied calmly.

He continued, "You just need to focus on your daily routine and you will be surprised to find out how much of your precious time you are wasting every day and every hour, unknowingly. We can easily create additional working hours for ourselves by simply utilizing this time."

"I always make a to-do list beforehand; schedule each and every appointment of mine. Each meeting, session, interaction and work hour, each and everything is meticulously planned beforehand, then where is the wasted time that you are talking about" I said in a little irritated tone.

I continued and said, "Your philosophy might be true for unorganized workers or people having limited knowledge or absolutely no knowledge of time management".

"It's not like that" He replied in a disapproving tone and continued, "I know this concept is new for you but it's a valid and working method which I have been teaching to my pupils over the years. I can easily prove it to you."

"Then please explain a little, how it works. Please forgive me if I may sound a little offensive, but your preposition seems to be too philosophical to be true." I said in a skeptical tone.

Professor smiled and said, "Theories need explanations but facts can be verified with experience." He paused for a while and asked after thinking a little, "Do you really want to check out the validity of my concept?"

"By all means" I replied instantly

 (Contrary to my expectations he was not at all offended when I expressed my disbelief in this philosophy, the level of confidence and the amount of conviction which he had in his concept intrigued me.)

"Ok, let me give you an assignment for today. But you will have to follow the instructions unabridged and honestly." He replied enthusiastically.

"An assignment....." I mumbled and then said thoughtfully, "Ok, I will do it, but hopefully it does not take much of my time as I won't be able to spare much of it."

Professor said laughingly, "Don't worry; it's not a college assignment."

It won't be wrong to say that he had my attention and I was fully interested in knowing what all he had to say.

"Tell me professor, what am I supposed to do. We are about to reach at the University" I asked inquisitively.

Professor replied, "As soon as you reach your office, just took out a piece of paper and start making a time log in it."

"A time-log, what is it? How to make it? You had promised that your assignment will not be tricky." I said as we reached in the university parking lot.

"It's simple, just pen down the task which you are doing and write the time of start and finish against the task" Professor said in an assuring tone.

As I stopped the car, professor said while opening the door, "And one more thing, don't forget to chart down the in-between interruptions along-with their time durations, no matter how small they might be.

Be it a washroom break, tea break or a little chit-chat with your colleague. Jot down each and everything along with its duration."

He closed the door and waved me goodbye. I turned the car and headed straight towards my office. As I was running late, so on my way to the office I had to honk at people on the streets so that they should just not tempt or even think about crossing in front of my car.

Had jumped few red lights, one or two overtakes from the wrong side and finally I managed to reach the office and that on time!

Luckily, I was able to get the parking spot near front gate of the office building. I quickly parked my car, took out my stuff and entered inside the office building.

On my way to the security check, I meet my assistant manager Mac; he greeted me and said, "Good morning sir".

"Good morning, Mac" I replied back

He was looking a little irritated. I continued and asked, "What happened? Is everything fine with you?

I smiled and said candidly while placing my hand on his shoulder, "Cheer up! Don't you think it's too early to get angry? You have got the entire day with you for doing that."

He smiled a little and replied calmly, "Sir, traffic nowadays has become impossible. There is no respect left for stop light, zebra crossing or lane driving."

He continued as we walked pass the security, "You won't believe, I almost got killed today when one idiot jumped passed the red light and honked at me when I was about to use zebra crossing, somehow I managed to pull back in time."

It appeared as if he was narrating and cursing my driving style. It was a little embarrassing and I was feeling a little awkward too, so I tried to change the topic and asked him interrupting, "How is your fiancé, hope two of you enjoyed your weekend?"

"It was great; we had a lot of fun." He replied happily. Breaking out of his state of nostalgia he asked me, "how was your weekend sir?

"It was usual" I replied as we walked down the corridor.

I continued, "I had a guest, a professor of human psychology; he is a motivator too. He is going to stay with me for some time."

Mac said enthusiastically, "A motivator in house, this sounds great. It is always good to have company of such people. I have heard that these people charge hefty amounts for their speeches and classes."

"Sir, can you please ask him to deliver a guest lecture at our company auditorium, this may help to boast up the motivation level of our employees." Mac continued keenly.

I replied thoughtfully, "I was also thinking on these lines, I will talk to him in the evening and if everything goes well we will arrange it for Friday."

"That will be great sir", Mac said energetically.

We continued walking down the lobby, Mac was first to leave as his section was located midway in the lobby and I continued walking to my corner office.

On my way, I smiled a little while thinking about the professor's assignment. Frankly speaking, his assignment appeared a little childish to me. But, since I have promised him and moreover, I also wanted to see the outcome of his approach; so I decided to follow it meticulously.

As I entered my office, my secretary was quick to greet me. She took my bag and coat and placed them neatly at the designated spots.

I removed the cufflinks and folded the cuffs of the shirt a little and took out a paper. I glanced at my watch and quickly scribbled the time on it and placed it aside.

My secretary, who was already standing next to my chair holding the appointment diary in her hand, looked curiously at the paper but avoid commenting about it.

After making the first entry on the time-log, I asked my secretary, "So Stacy, what have you lined up for me today?"

Stacy was quick to respond and briefed me about the today's schedule. It was quite a busy one. After getting abreast about today's schedule, I asked Stacy to make me a cup of coffee whereas I opened my laptop to check for important mails.

The coffee machine was already on, so she quickly poured a cup of coffee for me and handed it to me after adding necessary amount of sugar and milk to it.

Meanwhile, I jotted down the time at which I started checking my emails on that paper and after going through my mails I made another entry in the time log as soon as I finished checking the emails.

Stacy looked inquisitively at me and at the piece of paper on which I was scribbling something, but still she avoided asking about it.

After checking my emails, I glanced at watch it was 10:30 am and I was scheduled to attend a meeting at 11:15 am. I looked at Stacy, she was busy typing something. I asked her, "Stacy, what are you typing?"

"Sir, I am typing the draft memo which you had dictated to me yesterday, for the upcoming motivation week" She replied as she continued typing.

I said thoughtfully, "How about calling a motivational speaker to the office? I was thinking about it."

"That would be great!" Stacy replied promptly.

Stacy paused a little and continued, "Sir, please don't mind me asking but from when you started listening to the motivators? As far as I remember, you find such lectures and speeches boring."

I replied changing the topic, "Oh nothing like that! I was simply thinking of doing something new this time. Don't you think typing and distributing this memorandum is a little boring as well as an obsolete idea."

"That's true sir. The idea of calling a motivator is very encouraging and delightful. In fact, I myself very much like listening to the motivators. They are awesome and......."

I said while interrupting this unfazed and enthusiastic speech of my secretary, "Stacy, hold your horses. It's just an idea, nothing has been finalized yet. Let's see how things unfold."

Realizing her over enthusiastic approach and elated tone, she blushes a little and said apologizing in a low tone, "Sorry sir, I got a little carried away."

"There is nothing to apologize, in fact it is good to know that you liked this idea and perhaps other employees might also like it" I said assuring her.

She looked at the watch and said hurriedly, "Sir, it's almost 11:10 am I think we should hurry up for the meeting"

I quickly got up from the chair, arranged my cufflinks and said while putting on the coat, "Have you kept all the necessary documents?"

"Yes sir" Stacy replied as she picked up a neatly tied folder from the table.

We quickly left the room and paced our way to the conference hall. Thankfully, we managed to get in minutes before the meeting started.

After meeting was over, we walked to our room while discussing the important agenda points on our way. As we entered the room, I quickly took out the log sheet and scribbled the time on it. This time, Stacy mustered some courage and said, "Sir, please don't mind me asking but I have noticed that since morning you are scribbling down something on a piece of paper. What is it?"

I replied smilingly, "Nothing, it's just a little assignment from a professor."

Sensing her confusion, I said, "Don't worry, I will explain it to you later. Now let us focus on the work that has been assigned to our unit in the meeting."

"Sure sir" replied Stacy. The curiosity was very much evident on her face but I decided to ignore it and we continued with our work.

In this way, by the end of day I have successfully created the time-log sheet which professor had asked me to do?

Surprisingly, today I was eager to go home and show the sheet to the professor. I smiled at my naivety and headed towards the car parking. When I was about to unlock my car's door, Stacy waved at me from the gate and came tiptoeing towards me, in her high heels.

As she came closer I asked her, "Stacy what happened?"

She placed her hand on the car's boot and said after catching her breath, "Sir, my brother was supposed to pick me up today but he is stuck at work. Would you mind dropping me to the nearest metro station?"

"Why don't you learn to drive? I said as I unlocked the car.

I said after placing my bag on the car seat, "Come on, and hop in".

Stacy swiftly got seated inside the car and she quickly put on the seat belt.

I said while wearing seat belt, "Don't worry, I will drop you at your home."

"Oh no...no.... Sir, you don't have to take this much of trouble for me. Just drop me at the metro station and I will manage after that" Stacy replied hastily.

I said as we drove out of the parking, "It's nothing like that. Today, I am heading straight to my home instead of club."

I took a quick glance at her and said, "As far as I remember, you live somewhere near my home. I can easily drop you at your home. So sit back and relax."

While driving on the highway I asked her, "Stacy, why don't you learn to drive. Driving has become a necessity nowadays."

Stacy replied while holding the seat belt with both of her hands, "I tried learning but it's not my cup of tea."

"Why so?" I asked surprised.

Stacy replied in a humble tone, "I don't know. But whenever I sit behind the wheels my limbs become numb and frozen. My legs feel a ton heavier and difficult to move."

She took a deep breath and continued, "I don't know but I think my anxiety impairs my ability to drive"

I said assuring, "It is ok Stacy, don't go hard on you. I know you are very talented and will surely learn it soon."

She took a heavy breath and replied with a dull tone, "Sir, thanks for having faith in me. But I don't think driving is for me but I will still try to learn it."

After a little while, we reached at her home. She thanked me and even invited me over for a cup of tea but I humbly thanked her for her offer and drove away.

After another 5 min drive I reached my home. Parked the vehicle on porch and moved inside the house.

I asked Jerry who was busy preparing dinner, "Where is professor, is he back yet?"

Jerry wished me and said while serving me a glass of water, "Sir, he is in study"

I took out the paper from front pocket of my office bag and then placed the bag on a side table in the lobby and walked straight to the study. The professor appeared to be working on something. I cleared my throat to get his attention and then said, "Hello professor, hope I am not disturbing you?"

"Not at all, in fact I have already finished with the today's work" he replied as he carefully closed his fountain pen and placed it inside a flexible pen case.

He turned towards me and asked, "So, how was your day?"

"It was just a regular office day." I replied as I pulled the chair to sit across the professor.

I said while looking at the notes which professor had prepared, "it seems that you had quite a productive day."

"We can say that" professor replied candidly.

I placed the paper on the table and said, "Here is the assignment which you gave to me. Now tell me how we can make the time."

"That's quite impressive. Let's see what have you prepared." He said as he started to carefully scrutinize the document

9:30 - reached office

10:00 – 10:30 checked emails

11:15 – 12:35 meeting with senior officials

2:45-3:50 meeting with clients

4:00 – 5:20 team meeting

5:45 left office.

He placed that paper in a folder and said while looking at me, "That's good, but you forgot to mention details of in between breaks."

I asked him, "I don't take long breaks. But if you need them I can chart them for you tomorrow onwards."

"That would be perfect" replied professor.

I asked him, "Now tell me professor, how to make time?"

Professor looked at me and said in a serious tone, "I think we should wait till weekend"

The professor sounded quite serious with this assignment so I decided to wait till weekend. There was nothing to lose for me in this exercise. On the contrary, if it is really possible to make time then I don't think it would be harmful to learn that stuff.

From this moment onwards for next 5 days I meticulously documented the time log for each day and handed it over to the professor at the end of day. The professor would carefully scrutinize it and would simply place it inside the folder. Today was the Saturday, the last day of my assignment.

As soon as I handed over the time log sheet to the professor in the evening, I said, "Professor now tell me, what did we learnt from this assignment of yours?"

I continued and asked, "Tell me, how to make time?"

Professor took out all of the time log sheets from the folder and said as he placed them neatly on the table, "now careful look at all of them, one by one and tell me what you can infer by studying them?"

Monday

9:30 - reached office

10:00 – 10:30 checked emails

11:15 – 12:35 meeting with senior officials'

2:45 - 3:50 meeting with client

4:00 – 5:20 team meeting

5:45 left office.

Tuesday

9:35 - reached office

10:00 – 10:30 checked emails

11:15 – 12:30 client call

1 – 2 lunch break

2:25 – 3:15 team meeting

4:00 - 5:40 office work

5:45 left office

Wednesday

9:25 - reached office

10:00 – 10:30 checked emails

11:00 – 12:35 client call

1:00 – 2:00 lunch

2:35- 3:20 client meeting

3:45-4:50 team meeting

5:10 – 5:40 office work

5:45 left office.

Thursday

9:30 - reached office

10:00 – 10:30 checked emails

11:00 – 11:35 client call

Tea break

12:00 – 12:40 team meeting

1:00- 2:00 lunch break

2:45-3:50 meeting with clients

4:00 – 5:20 office work

5:45 left office

<table>
<tr><td>Friday</td><td>Saturday</td></tr>
<tr><td>9:30 - reached office</td><td>9:20 - reached office</td></tr>
<tr><td>10:00 - 10:30 checked emails</td><td>10:00 - 10:30 checked emails</td></tr>
<tr><td>11:15 -12:35 meeting with senior officials</td><td>11:00 - 12:30 meeting with vendors</td></tr>
<tr><td>1:00 - 2:00 lunch break</td><td>1:00 - 2:00 lunch break</td></tr>
<tr><td>4:00 - 5:20 team meeting</td><td>4:00 - 4:30 team meeting</td></tr>
<tr><td>5:45 left office</td><td>4:50 - 5:40 office work</td></tr>
<tr><td></td><td>5:45 left office</td></tr>
</table>

I carefully studied all of the time logs and said, "They look perfectly fine to me. All of the assigned tasks were accomplished successfully and that too in a time bound manner."

I said proudly as I looked towards the professor, "I had told you earlier, I am good at planning my work."

I pulled a chair for me and said while sitting on it, "Professor, I still can't understand how this exercise can help me to understand your concept of making the time."

"You will, my dear" professor said as he moved closer to the papers which were lying on the table.

He took out his pencil and started to mark on papers and after scribbling a little on them he said, "According to you, this was all the time in your hand which you could have utilized in a day."

"Yes, it was. Moreover, you should also appreciate the amount of work which I have completed in a single working day." I said while replying to his question.

He said while showing me the marking which he had made on the papers, "Please look carefully, now I will tell you how much more working hours you had at your disposal which almost went unnoticed, if not unused."

I was surprised to hear that. Sensing my state of mind, he continued without waiting for my response and said, "Let us start with one time log sheet at a time"

He picked up the time log for Monday and quickly scribbled something on it and I was keenly observing what he was writing on the papers

Monday	Tuesday
9:30 - reached office]30mins	9:35 - reached office
10:00 – 10:30 checked emails]45mins	10:00 – 10:30 checked emails
11:15 – 12:35 meeting with senior officials'	11:15 – 12:30 client call
2:45 - 3:50 meeting with clients 25+45 =70mins	1 – 2 lunch break
4:00 – 5:20 team meeting	2:25 – 3:15 team meeting
5:45 left office. 10+25=35mis	4:00 - 4:45 office work
	5:45 left office

Total=30+45+70+35=180mins = 3hours

Tuesday

9:35 - reached office

10:00 – 10:30 checked emails } 25mins

11:15 – 12:30 client call } 45mins

1 –2 lunch break } 30mins

2:25 – 3:15 team meeting } 25mins

4:00 - 5:40 office work } 45mins

5:45 left office   total=25+45+30+25+45=170mins

Wednesday

9:25 - reached office

10:00 – 10:30 checked emails } 35mins

11:00 – 12:35 client call } 30mins

1:00 – 2:00 lunch } 25mins

2:35- 3:20 client meeting   35mins

3:45–4:50 team meeting } 25mins

5:10 – 5:40 office work } 20mins

5:45 left office.   Total= 35+30+25+35+25+20=170 min.

After scrutinizing first few log sheets he said to me, "I have examined your time logs for 3 consecutive days and they show that invariably you have an unutilized time of about 3 hours or so in your hands on daily basis. Amazingly, you are absolutely unaware of this time. Aren't you"?

I was speechless in front of the evidence which professor presented to me. I held the time logs in my hands and was looking at them astonishingly without uttering a word.

He placed his hand on my shoulder and said, "I think, I have clearly explained to you what I mean by making time. It's simply being able to tap and utilize the time to the fullest. So that not even a single minute in a day is spent unknowingly"

For a moment nothing significant came to my mind. However, after taking few seconds to analyze what has just happened, I placed all of the time log sheets on the table and said, "I don't think, it's quite practical to practice what you are suggesting."

"What made you think so?" asked professor

I said in a firm tone, "I mean there is one thing called state of mind. You will have to accept that it plays a significant role in the way we perform and execute any task beforehand."

"Yes it does" he replied calmly

I continued and asked, "Then tell me, how I am supposed to utilize this unacknowledged time which you have just pointed out in these time logs. Especially when there are other important works scheduled before and after these time periods."

I paused for a little and said, "I mean to say that everyone needs a little time to prepare before an important client meeting or a presentation. How is it possible for me or anyone to get engaged in any other task before meeting? Is it not going to affect my state of mind?"

He said smilingly, "You are absolutely right. Such activities affect our state of mind but in a positive way, except for those who are always running behind in their schedules and are in habit of putting in last minute efforts."

"How a distraction can have a positive effect?" I asked curiously.

He replied, "Firstly, what I am suggesting to you is the optimum utilization of your working hours at your work place.

Secondly, I am not recommending you to involve in any leisurely or pleasure seeking activity; in fact, I am suggesting you to develop a habit of doing less productive and less demanding routine office jobs in these time periods or intervals. A little distraction is always useful in reducing the stress levels and anxiety."

He continued and said, "There are several trivial tasks in day to day office works which often gets neglected or delayed due to paucity of time. Works such as proper archiving of important papers, documentations, replying to less important mails or making follow up or courtesy calls to important contacts and clients often get delayed or neglected simply due to paucity of time. This list is endless."

"Therefore, by developing this habit of doing these trivial looking less important but relevant tasks during these unused times spells, you will not only increase your overall productivity but will also suitably address the subtle anxiety and stress which often precedes any big meeting or event."

He continued and said, "You were earlier talking about the state of mind. To maintain a perfect state of mind you need to learn to master your thinking process, because our state of mind is controlled by our thinking process. Thinking process is itself an elaborated issue and we will talk about it later"

However, coming back to your time log sheets, you can easily make out for yourself that you have a lot of unutilized time in your hand.

With your point regarding important meeting, I believe that if you have done your homework properly then there is nothing to worry about. Always remember a relaxed and calm mind thinks much faster, better and efficiently.

To further explain about this concept of state of mind, I will give you a very simple example which is relevant and in fact at some point of time, we all have experienced it personally.

Do you remember your school days? In school, all of the students are supposed to study and abide by the school timetable. Most of these timetables have back to back classes of only 30 to 45 minutes. At least 4 to 5 classes of different subjects are done back to back without any break in between them.

Now going by your excuse of the state of mind, a student should not be able to study math after doing a science or a literature class. They must be given a break of few minutes to centre themselves and arrive at a correct state of mind, isn't it?"

How is it so, that such young kids are not only able to understand and learn different subjects back to back but also appears in their class tests which are often conducted without giving them a break beforehand? A test or exam to a student is what a meeting is for a corporate.

How is it so? That a young student is able to handle all of this but a grownup individual is not?

All of this difference is due to the state of mind. A student knows it better that no one is going to listen to his excuses, so he develops his thought process and state of mind accordingly and as a result he is able to achieve and execute a lot and that too in a very limited period of time.

Whereas a grown up individual like you, who is far intelligent, mature and resourceful than a young student is finding it difficult to execute the tasks efficiently.

This is what the state of mind is capable of doing. Therefore, in order to develop a correct state of mind, first we need to work on and subsequently regulate our thinking process."

Always remember only ill prepared people are distracted. The person having a focused approach in life is always able to maintain a balanced state of mind.

He stood up from the chair and said after removing his reading glasses, "The time is the only currency which god gives to us. It's up to us how we spend it. A time spent wisely is the best investment a person can make in his life. At the end of day we all need time to do each and everything in our lives."

After completing his statement, he paused for a moment and said after thinking for a while, "One more thing; please don't confuse the concept of making time with micro management. Because here we are not dictating or controlling anyone else rather we are trying to encourage and discipline ourselves to maximize the utilization of time available with us."

Now I realized, he was right in the sense that 24hours in a day is a sufficient amount of time, provided we know how to manage it and even how to create additional time for ourselves.

No matter how much busy we think we are; we always have that unacknowledged and unnoticed time with us, which we often let go off without utilizing and cherishing it.

....✳✳✳..

What to do?

(This exercise is meant for the people who respect time and understand its importance in one's life)

Till now, we all have made, to – do lists, reminder diaries and some of us even have a well prepared bucket list. However, due to the paucity of time we often fail to execute these lists successfully.

Therefore, today let us learn to prepare another important list i.e. the time log sheet, which if prepared and practiced perfectly will enable us to execute all of the remaining lists that we have made for ourselves.

Remember, we need time to accomplish anything and everything in our life.

Let's see how to make a time-log sheet:

Keep a diary or note pad handy with you and make entries in following time log sheet template:

☞ **Time log sheet template**

(The first thing which you must do after getting up in the morning is to make an opening time-log entry in it)

I) your wake up time.....................................

The time when you actually left the bed............................

II) Time duration for which you used your wash room ....

III) Time you spend on your cell phone in morning hours...................

IV) Time you took for preparing and having your breakfast...............

V) At what time you actually left for your office...............................

VI) (A) When you reached in your office ....

(b) Actual time at which you reached your office............................

VII) (A) Time at which you started doing your first task of the day............

(b) Time at which you finished that task............................

VIII) (A) The duration of breaks which you took in-between the task...................

(b) The duration of actual break which you took in-between the task.........

IX) (A) The time of start of the next task...................

(b) The time of completion of that task.................

X) (A) The time you spent showing your work to the senior.....................

(b) Actual time you spent showing your work to the senior...............

XI) (A) Time you spent on your lunch break.............

(b) Actual time you spent on your lunch break....................

XII) (A) Time you spent on the subsequent tasks which you executed till the evening/end of your working day...................

(b) Actual time which you spent working on the subsequent tasks till the end of your working day...............................

XIII) In case of overtime or late sittings

(a) The time spent doing work......................

(b) Actual time spent doing work................

XIV) In case you go to the gym or exercising in the evening then

(a) The time spent in gym or exercising..................

(b) Actual time spent in gym or exercising.................

After having your dinner you should invariably examine this time log sheet at least for one complete month.

☞ **Now let us discuss the relevance of all the points which we have included in our time log sheet template, so that we can better understand the importance of this exercise and learn how it can benefit us.**

I. The actual wake up time will help us in understanding our actual snooze time, i.e. the time which we take from setting off the alarm and finally getting up and leaving the bed.

II. The time spent is bathroom:

It might appear irrelevant to most of us but it is of extreme relevance to some of us who are extremely hygiene conscious. Maintaining proper hygiene is a must but at the same time if done indiscriminately, this habits lead to Obsessive Compulsive Disorder. Therefore, we must be aware of how much time we are spending in our restroom.

Analysis of this time can help us to realize how much of the excess time we are wasting on daily basis, moreover repeated realization of this might also acts as a motivation forcing us to act to curb our obsessions (OCD).

III. Time spent on cell phone in morning hours;

Checking cell phone has become a norm in today's world and we can't avoid or ignore it. Even professionally it is almost impossible to completely stay away from our phones and other gadgets but by making time log we will be able to actually find out the time duration for which we are using our phone.

Analysis of this time will help us to quantify the approximate amount of screen time that we actually require in morning hours to fulfill our professional liabilities. This awareness can help us in saving a considerable amount of time in morning hours which can easily be utilized for self grooming.

IV. The time spent on cooking and having your meal.

Analysis of this time helps us understand how much attention we actually pay towards our health. In case, we are not able to have a proper breakfast then we really need to work out our morning schedule properly.

V. Monitoring of travel time:

By monitoring our actual travel time, we can opt for alternate routes or modes of transport, if possible.

Analysis of this time can help us to re-route and in case there is no other route available then we might be able to adjust our time of journey. Even a few minutes of head start in the time can have a significant effect on the traffic which we are going to face en route.

VI. The time of reaching office:

The time at we reached office is the time when we have punched in our card in the reader machine.

Whereas the actual time of reaching office is when we have settled ourselves in our seat or desk and are ready to work.

Analysis of this time will help us to estimate the amount of time which we require to actually settle in after reaching the office.

VII. Time taken to complete a task:

The actual time taken for completion of the task will help us understand how much time of the day we have actually spent on accomplishing the allotted task.

This is a very useful tool for self assessment as it helps us in quantifying the amount of time which we require to execute a specific type of job.

This knowledge helps us in planning and scheduling the future assignments in a realistically achievable manner.

VIII. Duration of breaks:

Duration of breaks stands for the multiple interruptions which we encounter during our task; it can be a little chit chat with a co-worker or going for supplies or may be a quick trip to smoking area.

It includes every unnecessary and unrequired interruption which interferes in the timely and proper execution of the work.

Such multiple interruptions often alter our flow of thoughts and the level of concentration, thereby making our work prone to mistakes and omissions.

Whereas, the actual break is the specified breaks which we take during specified time intervals during our day's work.

The analysis of break time helps us to understand what all elements or possible reasons exists which might be affecting our efficiency and the quality of our work.

This analysis will also help us to quantify our breaks in terms of time.

IX. The time spent on lunch break:

The time spent on lunch break is the total duration of the official lunch break. However, the actual time spent on the lunch break is the time which you actively utilize for having your meal.

Analysis of this time gives us an insight about the way we use our lunch time. This not only gives us an idea about the time which we exactly need to have our meal comfortably but it also gives us an insight of our approach towards our own health.

If we are not finding enough time to have our meal properly or if all the other trivial matters are consuming a majority portion of our lunch time then it clearly indicates that we are not giving proper attention to our health.

Unless or until we are sitting in an active ongoing meeting, we must not compromise on our lunch. To stay healthy we need to take meals at proper time.

It is far better to spare few minutes at appropriate time to have your meal rather than exposing our bodies to a number of life style diseases.

All we need is time, a health body and active mind to achieve success and happiness in life.

X. Time spent on showing your work to the senior:

It is the total time which we spend from getting up from our seat with the purpose of showing our work to the senior and returning back to our seat after submitting our work.

If the task is to be submitted and discussed online then the entire duration of the call will be considered for this purpose.

Whereas, the Actual time spent will be the time which was utilized purely for discussing the work related issue.

It is often observed that people tend to establish rapport with their seniors/ juniors on pretext of showing/ discussing some file or project.

It is good for networking but at the same time it is costing us dearly in terms of our time.

Because, what has been observed is that after few initial interactions, where we deliberately tend to talk about random issues of common interest to build a rapport with our superior officer, we find it difficult to cut short these unnecessary conversations which gradually starts becoming a norm of our interaction with our senior.

Analysis of this time gives us a true insight of how much of our productive time we are spending on discussing our work and how much on liaisoning.

Liaisoning is good for developing your rapport and business but care must be taken to ensure that we are not ending up in wasting a considerable chunk of our working hours in liaisoning instead of focusing on our work.

If this happens routinely then in order to compensate for the loss of time we need to increase our late sittings or the quality of our work gets undermined and unfortunately both of these situations are not in the best of our interest.

XI. Time spent on subsequent tasks:

It is the time which we spent on doing all of the other tasks which we are supposed to complete by the end of the day. Whereas the actual time is the time which was needed in reality to complete those tasks properly and satisfactorily.

Analysis of this time gives us quite clearer and overall picture of how we are utilizing our working hours in a given day. This analysis helps us to appreciate how much we have achieved in a day and what more we could have easily achieved, if we were wise enough in spending our time meticulously during the day.

XII. Time spent during late sitting or overtime:

It is the duration of time which we spent in office after normal office hours to complete few of the time bound tasks which are supposed to be finished by the end of the day or before next morning.

The actual time spent during late sitting is the time that was truly required to finish up that additional work.

Analysis of this time gives us an insight about the actual time which was truly needed by us to accomplish that task for which we had stayed late in the office.

We need to quantify the time which was actually needed to handle the task which we had completed during late sitting.

This will help us to figure out, whether it was possible to us to complete the task during routine working hours?

XIII. Time spent in gym: This time is also required to be monitored carefully.

We must refrain from indulging in gossips or chit chats with our gym buddy, while we are inside the gym. Rather, we must ensure that we are doing our workout with full strength and focus. Then only our efforts in gym are going to yield results.

Analysis of this time will help us understand why we are not able to achieve the desired results even after doing regular workouts.

Because when we focus more on the other less relevant things while doing our workout, it is quite normal to lose the count of reps or even miss out few of the exercises from the routine.

Due of this diverted attention our mind often fails to recognize the efforts put in by the body.

Realization is the first step towards improvement and when realization is absent, it become very difficult to improve and stay motivated.

At the end of the day after having your dinner you should invariably examine this time log sheet at least for one complete month, before going to bed.

When you will do this exercise honestly, you will be able to appreciate how much time you are spending unacknowledged and unutilized in a day.

☞ **How to avoid the time loss:**

In order to avoid time loss, first we need to identify the situations which are leading to the time loss. For this purpose we should begin with the analysis of our time log sheet.

For simplification, a format is given below for the analysis of the time log sheet.

<u>Analysis of the time log sheet:</u>

After doing thorough examination of the time log sheet you should summarize your day and write down the events which lead to the time wastage in following format:

Date	Event or the circumstances which lead to the loss of working hours	Total duration of time that was wasted	Was it preventable?	Your opinion on how you could have handled the situation better?	Remarks

Careful scrutiny of the entries made in the above analysis table will make is easy for you to pin point the reasons behind your underperformance at work place, or why do you feel overburdened.

Once you are fully aware of the circumstances or the reasons which are not allowing you to give your 100% at work, then surely you would be able to figure out a way to handle the situation which is resulting in the loss of working hours.

In fact, if efforts are put in to plug these time leakages then the requirement for late sittings or overtime will be seldom, which will further enhance the quality of your life.

With a little modification, the time log sheet template can be easily customized as per the needs and the requirements of the individual who wants to practice the concept of 'making the time'.

☞ **Steps to handle and avoid time leaks:**

We are supposed to pay equal attention to the fact that alongside the time management, we also need to maintain warm and cordial relations with our coworkers and seniors.

We cannot simply ignore every other aspect of the professional social life only to maximize the utilization of working hours. Therefore in order to strike a balance, following points are suggested for consideration:

1. Give priority to your work.

2. Greet people enthusiastically and politely, as this will help you in developing good rapport with the colleagues and that too in less time.

3. Talk precisely and avoid protracted conversations, especially when the necessary message can be conveyed in a few lines. This will save your time and energy.

4. You must not talk hastily and should maintain proper eye contact and a positive body language, so that you are better able to connect with the people.

5. Avoid taking unnecessary breaks.

***

Chapter-3

(Motivation)

"Trust yourself more than fearing others"

I Was absolutely impressed by the impeccable way with which he had explained the concept of making time. It took him only few minutes to tear apart all of my excuses for not utilizing my time efficiently and properly.

I asked professor as I stood up from the chair and walked towards the kitchen, "Would you like to have a cup of tea or coffee may be?"

"I would have a cup of coffee, please" replied professor.

I switched on the coffee machine; meanwhile professor was busy arranging his dairy and other important documents in his executive bag.

When done, he kept the bag on the study table and said while placing his reading glasses in his coat's pocket, "I hope you would be able to manage your time more efficiently now."

I smiled and said while pouring the coffee in cups, "Sure, it was a truly enlightening conversation to have."

I continued and said after handing over a cup to him, "How is your research work going?"

"It is going good. I have already interviewed around 30 volunteers but to my disappointment, majority of them are lacking in motivation. They are simply doing their jobs without any sense of belongingness or desire for excellence." Professor replied in a concerned tone while placing the cup on the table.

He paused for a while and continued after adding two cubes of sugar to his coffee, "No doubt, all of them were hard working, sincere and intelligent people but unfortunately most of them have a negative attitude towards life."

I said as I placed my cup on the table, "Impulsive nature, illogical thinking and directionless approach often make a person to behave weirdly."

On listening to my statement his expressions changed from being thoughtful to amazed, it was evident from his expressions that he was not expecting such a serious and meaningful statement from me.

"That's very true" he replied promptly.

Sensing this to be an appropriate opportunity, I said, "Professor, can I ask a favor from you?"

"Go ahead" he replied instantly.

I said, "Our office is organizing a motivation week as a part of team building exercise. Will it be possible for you to spare some time and deliver a lecture on motivation to the employees of our organization?"

"I would love to do that, tell me when I need to deliver that speech?" he said as he took out his appointment diary from his coat's pocket.

"Around 10:30am, this Friday." I replied instantly

While he was noting down the date and time on his appointment diary I asked inquiringly, "Professor, how much do you charge for such events?"

He smiled and replied calmly, "I won't charge from you".

I said interrupting, "No…no…no… that's not fair. I mean, I highly appreciate your gesture but since this is a company event and I don't see any reason for which you should do it for free. Moreover, if company does not have to pay for your time and knowledge then I am afraid that they are not going to pay appropriate attention towards you and your content."

Professor smiled a little and said while looking at me, "You are a considerate young man."

He took out his business card and said while handing it over to me, "This is me. You can pay me whatever you think is payable as per your company budget and policy"

"Fair enough" I said as I took the card from his hand.

Next morning, in the office, I decided to brief my team about the concept of 'making time'. I called all of the team members to the conference room and after briefing them about the concept and its rationale, I asked all of them to make a time log sheet at least for next 15 days.

This new concept generated mixed reactions from the team members but was warmly accepted by Stacy and Mac. Both of them are highly competitive and hardworking personnel, especially when compared to the rest of the team members.

After the team meeting, on our way back to the office, I said while handing over the professor's business card to the Stacy, "He will be our guest speaker for tomorrow's event?"

Her expressions changed from being skeptical to admiration. She asked astonishingly after reading the card, "Oh my god! I have read all of his books. Sir, how did you managed to get hold of him?"

Baffled by her reaction, I asked surprisingly, "What do you mean?"

Still riding high in her state of ecstasy she replied, "Sir, Mr. John is one of the best and most popular motivational speaker of all time. He has written many books and is actively involved in many motivational workshops."

I unlocked the office door and Stacy continued as we stepped inside the office, "It is very hard to get him"

She slightly inclined towards me and said almost whispering, "Even some of the officials in our top management are big fan of him."

"By making this happen, you have absolutely nailed your promotion. What a masterstroke!" She said while finally regaining her composure.

I was surprised and elated equally. I never knew that I was residing with such an accomplished celebrity. Had I not shared his card with Stacy today, his simplicity and humbleness would have never allowed me to guess about him?

"Stacy, do you have any idea about how much he might charge for this interaction?" I asked her doubtfully

"In fact lesser know speakers are charging 15-20K. I am sure, he must be charging well above 80K."She said affirming.

"What! 80k for a single session" I reiterated surprisingly.

Stacy said assuring, "Don't worry sir; management won't say a word about this. Even they also want to meet him, listen to him"

Suddenly her tone and expressions changed from being elated to skeptical and she asked inquiringly, "Sir, haven't you discussed about his fees yet?"

I replied calmly, "No, but he has confirmed the appointment"

She said assuring, "Don't worry, you can contact his staff and they will let you know about the details. Then we can take up the matter with the management"

She walked towards the phone and said while holding his business card in her hands, "Do you want to me call? I can ask them for the details"

"No thanks Stacy, I think I will talk to him on his cell phone" I replied while reaching for my mobile phone on the table.

Stacy asked surprisingly, "but sir, it is not mentioned on the business card. All I see is landline numbers, fax numbers, emails but no mobile number. From where did you get his mobile no.?"

"From him, because he is presently living with me" I replied as I called professor on his mobile phone.

Stacy was looking at me awestruck, it was quite understandable. Meanwhile, I had the conversation with professor and he agreed for any amount that I think is appropriate for the event.

I knew I had to share few details with Stacy to curb her curiosity. So I briefly told her about last few days and how I have unknowingly befriended one of the humblest and knowledgeable old man who is, according to the Stacy, one of the best motivator around. Then I asked her to confirm regarding his charges from his staff.

Stacy quickly called on the number given on the business card and we came to know that he charges 90K for each session.

After this I approached the higher management and just as Stacy had predicted they were ready to pay any amount to have the professor in the office and interact with him.

Next morning everyone in the office was eager to meet professor. For most of my colleagues and staff, it was a new experience to meet a motivator.

Till today, all of us had heard long lectures on deadlines, targets and company policies. Often, these lectures are followed by inevitable subtle ruthless verbal bashing of few staff members.

Therefore, today's interaction was expected to be a little different, wherein we might get to listen to something new that might really help us to improve, grow and become successful. The best part of today's interaction was that no one is going to scold anyone at the end of interaction.

I entered into the auditorium along with the professor, introduced him to the top company brass and then escorted him to his seat.

From C.E.O to Directors all were giving speeches one after another simply to show off their level of intelligence and knowledge. However, this time they were concise.

Finally our VP invited the professor on to the stage and handed over the microphone to him.

As he stepped in, the auditorium resonated loudly with the claps and cheers for him. He smiled and waved his hand towards the crowd and allowed them to settle on their own.

Once everyone calmed down, he started with his speech, "Dear friends, good morning and thank you for inviting me here and sparing your valuable time. Your enthusiasm has ensured that I am at the right place with right kind of people, the people who are energetic, enthusiastic and willing to learn and improve.

(During his speech, we was not standing at the dais but was continuously ambling to and fro on the stage)

Your willingness to learn is inciting me to start the lecture with out wasting a single minute" (*his words put smile on the face of audience and now they were all ears to him.*)

He walked towards the dais, opened a water bottle and said after quickly gulping it down, "Friends, I am really happy at this initiative of yours to celebrate a motivation week. Today, I would also share some of my thoughts on motivation and how can you stay motivated in life.

But before going further, first we need to understand the exact meaning of motivation.

MOTIVATION

Motivation is a miraculous word that is associated with immense energy and vast potential.

It is the pivot around which our entire world of success, fame and glory revolves. It provides much needed healing to our aching heart, and immense power and resolute to our wandering mind.

> *It is the only word which has the potential to turn odor into the aroma. It is that spark which if ignited can transform a handicap into hero; it makes the blind to feel what a person with eyes might fail to see.*

Motivation, it makes the best out of us and encourage us to do what was considered impossible by us before.

It is one of the most commonly used words, with which we all are familiar. Still, it keeps on appearing regularly in newspapers, in books and in many of the lectures delivered by wise.

However, unfortunately this is the most vital trait, which many of us are lacking within. We are everything, but not motivated.

Even if a little bad or something unexpected happens to us, we panic immediately and consequently we became absolutely blank. Now we start thinking about all the possible but negative outcomes of that situation in particular.

> *Motivation is not about talking something big in front of others. It is just not about big words and world acclaimed phrases, which a person can tell to someone and then waits for his own turn to hear those soothing words and great success stories of legendary people, when he himself is down with failure and frustration.*

Just by telling the wonderful stories of some successful people, you cannot motivate a person or self.

However by doing so, surely you can induce a little phase of illusionary bravery, which will persist till that story or the stuff echoes in your ears. Once the sound is gone the thoughts will fade away soon from one's mind, leaving you back at the square 1.

Nobody can rise until he himself starts climbing; you ought to be a cliffhanger to scale the heights, just listening about the stories of trekking by others does not and will not serve the purpose.

Nobody wins until he wants to emerge out victorious.

Any external agent cannot motivate you; it is something, somewhere deep inside us, which when gets clicked make us do the miracles.

It can be anything, like meeting an old friend of yours who has made a lot of fortune in little time, or it can be an emotional suffering at individual level. I mean, it can be anything which can shake up your mind, soul, and heart.

Any event which is capable of forcing you to introspect carries an immense power to incite you to do what was earlier considered as impossible by you.

NOW QUESTION ARISES, "If a person lacks in motivation then do he has to wait for a disaster to happen or for a visit from an old friend, to become motivated in life".

No, it is not so!

If you lack in motivation, you can achieve it on your own and that too without any external help.

NOW QUESTION ARISES, "*If a person does not require any external agency to become motivated then why he remains latent?*"

There is absolutely no doubt in this point that you need no external agency for carrying out an internal change.

The external influences are often short-lived, because by the time they really start unsettling you, their own influence starts wearing away. Therefore, they cannot affect any substantial change in a person.

It is well said that, "Unless you feel that a change is necessary, you cannot change"

A person is latent until he does not immensely realize the need for the activity. Once you realize the need for an action then you execute it without caring about the consequences.

Because, at that moment you know what you are doing and no matter what people have to say about it, you put in your best efforts to get the job done and most of the times you got it done satisfactorily.

On other hand when external agents drive you. You lack the spirit of performance; therefore what you do then is just thinking and doing your best to pass the buck.

We all know that only by thinking about the job and not doing the necessary efforts won't yield any result, however, it simply adds to our frustration and further elongates the list of our failures.

Now Question Arises, "How To Remain Motivated In Life?"

Motivation is not a single entity; but it is the outcome of the combination of various traits being executed in harmony.

There are 11 traits or 11 secrets or we can call 11 steps which we need to follow and practice routinely to stay motivated in our life.

I would like to refer to them as 11 traits. Now, I want all of you to listen carefully and memorize all of these 11 traits, which are:

1. **Perseverance,**
2. **Faith in your own beliefs,**
3. **Logical analysis of situation,**
4. **Learn to manage your thinking process,**
5. **Develop your own vision:** which must be based on certain concrete yet logical and socially acceptable fundamentals,
6. **Stop brooding,**
7. **Stop acquiring sympathies:** Sympathies only weaken you further from inside and makes you to lose your credibility,
8. **Never be emotionally driven,**
9. **Self appreciation,**

10. **Never take situations personally:** Try to sort out and
understand the logic behind the events or situations,

11. **Never hesitate to accept your failure:** Always remember
even if you have failed then this is also just another result,

To stay motivated in life, first of all, we need to learn to focus our mind and channelize our energies to get the maximum out of our life.

If you were attentive enough to note down all of the 11 traits which I had just enumerated and are willing to work on these traits; than trust me you will be amazed to find that not a single point requires any outside influence or assistance.

I can say this with utmost commitment and sincerity that you have it in you, just practice to have faith in yourself, respect your decisions, strive hard to fulfill your commitments and do your best to meet the deadlines.

You are the only one, who can successfully lead yourself through the hurdles and obstacles of life.

People around will only trust you, when you will learn to trust yourself.

We all are here to work, to have good time and to add meaning to our lives.

Dear friends before concluding this lecture, I would reiterate, "We all are blessed with same virtues, as god does not differentiate among his children".

All we have to do is, "trust our self more than fearing others, and believe in our self more than believing others".

I have full faith and trust in you and your desire to succeed, and I will request you all to have same faith in yourself and in your abilities. Always remember that we all are equally blessed, just learn to explore your inner self and see the difference.

> *No one is perfect, the only difference between you and the person you are looking at is, that he is more organized, determined, devoted, hardworking, and committed than you are.*
>
> *If you want to beat him, just make yourself a bit more organized, a little bit more determined, slightly more devoted, and a little more hardworking and committed. Soon you will be able to see the difference in you, in your potential and in the position subsequently.*

Thank you very much for listening to me with this amount of patience and attention.

I am really honored and thankful to my young friend Patrick, who provided me with this opportunity to speak in front of such a lovely and enthusiastic crowd. Thank you very much!

With these words professor handed over the microphone to the stage coordinator and walked toward his seat. His lecture generated a huge round of applause.

Everyone in the office was talking about him, and his concept of 11 traits.

Even the CEO came to my cabin and appreciated me for arranging such an extraordinary speaker. I accepted his compliments and gradually become busy with my work. When the clock struck 6 pm, everyone started for their respective destinations.

Today after a long time, I was eager to reach home and meet the professor. His lecture has ignited an unfailing desire in me to learn more, mainly because of the two reasons:

Firstly, I was new to this motivational stuff and his lecture literally walked me through the least known path of my life.

I mean, I have rarely read any motivational book and neither do I prefer listening to the motivational speech or quotes.

Frankly speaking, I used to think that these speeches, quotes and books are purely meant for losers and especially for those who can't think rationally and decide for themselves.

But today, he not only proved me wrong but also changed my perspective towards motivation and the purpose of motivational content.

Secondly, I was already impressed by his result oriented approach. His last concept of 'making time' proved a lot beneficial for me; therefore, I was keen to learn few more useful and practical concepts from him.

......................................❋❋❋...

What to do?

Step -1: Make a list

First make a list of all the 11 traits and paste this list on the first page of the time log sheet file or diary, so that reading this list is the first thing, with which you start your day and the last thing to read before sleeping.

Step-2: Maintain Secrecy

When you start working on yourself, treat it like a top secret project and instead of boasting around, keep it to yourself.

This feeling of secrecy will give you the much needed push and an objective to accomplish your goals before anyone else came to know about them.

Even after putting in persistent efforts for few days, if you think that despite of all your efforts you are losing the track then subtly disclose your objective to one of your close friends in a very casual conversation.

It is not significant whether he/ she paid attention to your statement or not but for sure you will feel as if you have bared it all in front of him/ her and now you need to cover it up as fast as you can. This induced sense of urgency will provide you with the much needed reason to stay motivated and focused on your objective.

But priority must be given to keep your dreams and objectives close to your heart.

Step-3: Practice Inner Silence

Develop a habit of staying silent; this quality is a must to acquire a calm and composed state of mind.

By silence, I am referring to the inner silence. The silence inside our inner self helps us in attaining a conflict-free state of mind which is often open to all new possibilities.

Step-4: Let go of the past

To maintain the peaceful and silent state of mind, we need to let go of all the grudges, resentments and anguish.

In order to achieve this state of mind, try your best not to revisit any of your bad memories or rough patches of your life.

In case you are unable to do so due to any given reason, than ensure to change the perspective with which you revisit those memories.

Instead of looking at them as the ugly moments worth of self pity, you should try to focus what different you could have done at that moment and was it possible, at all, for you to act differently at that moment?

Gradually, you will understand that the choices which you had made at that moment in past, were the best which you could have made under those circumstances.

It is the circumstances which guide our choices and affect our mental abilities therefore, it is not wise and neither advisable to analyze a situation retrospectively, especially when we are not facing those circumstances presently, under which we had actually made those choices in the past.

Step-5: Learn to channelize your resources and abilities

Once by constant practice, when we have learnt to maintain this relaxed and conflict-free State of mind, we will be easily able to channelize all our resources and abilities to achieve our goals successfully.

Step-6: Inner peace

I have laid a significant emphasis on the inner peace and always consider it as one of the most important aspect to succeed in life, because it is these inner voices which cause the worst kind of trauma, anguish and stress to us, rather than any other external stimulus.

If you are able to silent these inner voices of distress, disbelief, uncertainty, insecurities and self-doubt then you have already marched few steps ahead in your life, towards attaining your goal.

Step-7: Learn to manage your thinking process

Learn to tame your thinking process, so that if you have to think at all, than you should only think about ways to make yourself prosperous, healthier, happier and successful.

We will talk in length about how to control our thinking process in later chapters.

....✿✿✿..

Chapter-4

(Perseverance and its importance)

"Perseverance is the soul of success."

I Parked my car on the porch and moved inside. On my way to the study, I placed my car keys on the key holder and my office bag on the side table.

As I walked pass the kitchen, I was surprised to see Professor donning a track suit. It was a little weird as I have always seen him wearing a suit.

I greeted him and said, "You are looking a bit different today."

"I just wanted to clear up my mind, so I am planning to take a brisk walk in the nearby park, will to like to join?" he asked as he walked towards the main door.

Finding this as an appropriate opportunity to learn something new from him, I replied, "Sure, just give me 5 and I will be with you"

"Ok take your time, I will wait for you" he said as he glanced at his wrist watch.

I quickly freshened up, changed my clothes to a bit more casual, had a glass of juice and walked out of the main door. Professor was standing in the drive way.

"That was really quick" professor said while glancing at his watch

I replied smilingly, "I am the man of my words".

"That's true" professor replied as we started walking towards the park which was located across my house. It took us few minutes to get in the park.

Contrary to what I had expected, he was a quiet walker. He had not uttered a word in last 20 minutes. By now, I was already tired and the fact that I was not able to extract anything relevant from him has further dampened my enthusiasm to walk.

I thought that he must be tired by now, so I peeked a little at him from the corner of my eyes, but to my surprise he was marching like a soldier.

My body has already started showing the sign of fatigue, which he was quick to notice. He said, "Please don't walk like a sloth. Keep your spine straight and head held high."

Without bothering for my response he continued, "I think you don't know that our body posture and our ability to handle stressful situations are interrelated."

That was surprising. "What our posture has to do with stress management", I thought to myself.

I asked him inquisitively, "How so? I have never heard about it"

He kept walking and replied, "Ok, let me explain this to you. Have you ever noticed that when a person fails to cope up with stress, his shoulders start dropping and face loses all the charisma and glow?

In-fact, a person exhibiting a positive body language is always more likely to get hired. Isn't?"

I nodded in affirmation.

He continued, "It is essential to maintain a positive body posture to develop a positive state of mind, especially when we are faced with a tough or demanding situation".

"I will keep this in mind and will surely work on my posture and body language. However, professor I want to ask you something?" I said

Professor walked towards a bench which was positioned alongside the walking track. He replied after comfortably sitting on it, "What do you want to know?"

"Your speech was excellent and I was closely following it. I agree with you on most of the points but I don't understand how perseverance is important to stay motivated.

Till now, I had an understanding that motivation leads to perseverance. It's fair to understand that a motivated person will do consistent efforts, till he succeeds.

But in your speech you have mentioned perseverance as one of the key traits to stay motivated. I am a little lost on this, would you please care to explain it further?" I asked him

Professor said smilingly, "I must admit, you are a very attentive young man. Ok, I will explain it to you but I have a condition?"

"A condition, what's that?" I asked curiously

He said, "You will not interrupt me in-between. If any question arises in your mind, you will hold it, till I am done with the topic."

I nodded in acceptance and he started with his answer,

"PERSEVERANCE AND ITS IMPORTANCE IN LIFE

It is often observed that we are not able to differentiate between **PERSEVERENCE** and **PASSION.**

To succeed in life what we truly need is perseverance and not the passion.

Frankly, there is no significant difference between passion and madness, as with madness, you are already mad; whereas, passion gradually drives you towards the madness.

Passion is never alone; in fact, it's a package deal. It is often accompanied by the frustration of failure. This frustration further forces us to feel low and inefficient.

This feeling of inefficiency often manifests as anger and restlessness, thereby further diminishing our chances of regaining composure and sanity.

Passion is just like a fire cracker which is going to create a lot of light, sound and an environment full of energy but just for a moment. Once it gets consumed, it's gone, leaving behind only smoke, ashes and darkness.

Passion without perseverance will drive you crazy. Having passion without perseverance is just like having a car with no fuel in it so that you can sit in it but cannot reach your destination.

Therefore, if you are passionate for something but do not possesses the quality of perseverance within you then you are playing with fire.

Under such circumstances, it is wise to leave the passion for a while.

It is a common misconception in society that, a passionate person makes a great winner out of him.

However, in reality, a passionate person lacking in perseverance, makes his life miserable, because his passion does not allow him to forget his dreams and overambitious goals, and the absence of perseverance in efforts does not allow him to achieve them.

Therefore, at the end of day, "He is totally a frustrated and exhausted person who is just adding stress to his life and in the life of people around him, day after day; which ultimately leads to the total failure".

NOW QUESTION ARISES, "Is it wrong to have a passion in life?"

No, it is not true completely. However, passion without perseverance is useless and undermining.

For example: if passion is to dream of achieving 100% marks in exams then perseverance is to study day and night towards achieving that goal.

(Although, what he said was quite unconventional but still his words were making sense to me. I always knew perseverance is important in life but I never took a deep thought on it. Till today, for me perseverance only had a literal meaning but professor made me realize that this word has got a lot more to it than just a literal meaning in a dictionary.)

Professor paused for a while and asked, "Do you have any questions so far? Or I may continue?"

"Is it possible to develop this trait? In case a person is lacking in it or simply doesn't have it at all." I asked hesitatingly

"Yes, it is possible to do so. We can cultivate this habit by following certain methods." Professor continued

These methods when followed religiously and with full commitment can lead to the measurable changes.

☞ **There are 4 points to practice:**

1.   AVOID UNNECESSERILY THINKING ABOUT WHAT YOU HAVE ALREADY PLANNED FOR YOUR FUTURE:

As repeated thinking will not only waste your time, but it will also provide you with multiple chances to think about the unexpected and unlikely failures.

We need to learn to tame our thinking process, so that we are able to wisely use the available time and resources in hand towards implementing what we have already planned, rather than just sitting idle and imagining for the worse.

Remember one thing that we are here to exert and emerge out as winners and not to get sacred by thinking only about obstacles and focusing on our limitations.

Therefore, avoid unnecessary thinking as it creates panic, wastes our precious time and energy, which we could have easily used otherwise in realizing our goals.

2. NEVER FIX EXACT GOALS:

Instead of fixing exact goals or targets, set a range thereby allowing yourself with a bit of flexibility.

Since we are human beings living in a society, therefore apart from professional life we also have some social responsibilities in life, which also need our time and attention. Sometimes due to these responsibilities, it becomes very difficult to meet those self-imposed fixed targets.

Failing to accomplish the target often leads to profound disappointment and self-disapproval; this further dampens our enthusiasm and often triggers a cycle of brooding and cynicism.

The frustration generated by these actions leads to the further loss of our valuable time, which sometimes amounts to days or even weeks.

On the contrary, if you have set a range of target instead of a fixed target for yourself to achieve, then you might save yourself from all this wastage of time and energy because it is possible to miss out a fixed target but it is hard to fall short of a flexible range.

It does not matter even if your performance falls at the lower end of the range; because still you get a feeling of accomplishment and a hope to perform better next time.

Moreover, this feeling is much better to have rather than the feelings of frustration and rejection, which we get at the end of the day when we fail to meet our fixed targets.

3.   DO REGULAR ASSESMENTS OF YOUR WORK BUT AVOID ANY THOROUGH EVALUATION IN BETWEEN:

Whenever we are working towards achieving a goal; we need to have a properly drafted and sorted out action plan along-with the willingness to work hard in order to execute our plan successfully.

Apart from these two requirements, it is always advisable to routinely assess our work in between, so that we should not become complacent and is able to maintain the steady pace of our work.

However, we must refrain from performing a detailed and thorough analysis of executed work midway. Because, if done so, it would not only lead to an unnecessary wastage of working hours but will also add unnecessary stress in case, we have failed to meet the target at each and every stage of our work.

This stress of the underperformance often leads to the frustration and sometimes even depression, which eventually slows down the speed of future progress and gradually everything comes to a grinding halt.

On the other hand, a slight amount of assessment encourages us and prompts us to do much better in future; as in this case, we are getting positive feedback of being able to do at least something meaningful towards fulfilling our larger goal and that too in the manner planned by us.

It has been observed that often people tend to overlook the quality of work when they are unable to meet the target on time. One must ensure that no compromise is being done with the quality of work merely to maintain a constant pace of work.

Remember it not the pace which matters, but it is the consistency in efforts, which is far more important. Pace can be variable.

If you are performing low today then there is every possibility that you can outperform yourself tomorrow and in the days to come.

Therefore, what is most important is to work regularly and this regularity in efforts is PERSEVERANCE.

4. DON'T WORRY ABOUT THE RESULTS:

A result is the collective outcome of several factors which are in play, when we are executing any task. Few of these factors can be controlled by us but at large most of them are not under our absolute control.

Therefore, we must not evaluate our worth especially with reference to the results in hand. Results are the part and parcel of any task and they should be treated accordingly.

This ability to remain uninfluenced by the results whatsoever they might be is the most important trait required to develop perseverance.

Because if we are going to assess ourselves and decide our worth merely on the basis of any single result, then I am sure we are expected to arrive at a flawed conclusion of under achievement.

This flawed conclusion will open the gateways to another time and energy consuming self depreciating analysis, which often ends up sucking away rest of our resources, in form of time and energy. The same resources which we could have easily used otherwise in doing damage control or working out a new but evolved action plan for us.

The point of paramount importance is to put in a wholehearted attempt without leaving any space for any excuse. You should give in your 100% or take the best possible shot, so that when the result comes, no matter what it is, you already know that this is all what you could have possibly done.

No matter what we plan to achieve, we should always make realistic and achievable goals and must not forget to leave some space for our personal and social commitments.

I can say with conviction that if you follow what I am contemplating on this topic then for sure, you will be a far better and a successful person at the end of the day.

So have patience, learn and practice perseverance in your life and you will achieve your goals successfully.

Professor said concluding, "Perseverance is the soul of success."

"This was truly enlightening" I replied.

Thereafter we chatted for a while and then walked back to the house.

....❋ ❋ ❋..

What to do?

☞ Step-1: Always maintain a correct posture

⇨ When you get up in the morning, walk up to the mirror and look at your posture. If it's not good then correct it.

⇨ Whenever you happen to come across any mirror just make it a point to notice your posture and correct it, if needed. Gradually, you will come to a point when you don't move an inch without a proper posture.

⇨ Posture plays a significant role in determining the way our mind is going to perceive our self. Posture tells a lot about our state of alertness, presence of mind and confidence level.

☞ Step -2: Always start with setting realistic and achievable goals.

⇨ Just as in case of a new born baby, when he gradually grows up and learns to walk he begins with crawling and passes several in between stages over a period of time before his is finally able to walk without any support.

⇨ Now, would it be possible for the baby to directly start running no matter how much motivation, knowledge and support is provided to him? No, he won't be able to do that instead he might develop the tendency of self doubt and feeling of insufficiency in later life.

⇨ Therefore, always remember to begin with achievable and realistic goals which can be accomplished in available or manageable resources.

⇨ Just like Growth, success is also a continuous process. To be successful in life, you need to be successful consistently. A success on few occasions will not truly serve the purpose.

☞ **Step-3: To stay perseverant you must not be influenced by the results**

⇨ No matter how good, bad or even worse the results might be in some situations. Always remember that results are nothing more than the indicators conveying the percentage of necessary information, knowledge or expertise which you currently possess.

⇨ Therefore, there is nothing to feel bad about them. Just focus on how much you have learnt and how much more is needed to be learnt.

⇨ Instead of making hue and cry on failing and tearing down oneself in distress, simply focus on what percent of knowledge is required to be learnt to get the job done successfully.

....❈ ❈ ❈..

Chapter-5

(Problem Solving &
The Concept of Fact Assessment Sheet)

"The solution always lies within us but we often stray out in search of it".

Next morning, I woke up a little early. I was feeling much energetic and relaxed. Today, I was not in a rush. I walked out of my room to the lawn.

On every holiday, I like to have my morning tea served to me in my garden. (This is the only time in the entire week when I can relax and spend few moments of my life doing nothing but enjoying my surroundings. In fact, this is the only reason for which I never sold my ancestral home to buy a flat in some swanky high rise apartment, which most of my friends have.)

The professor was already up and he was walking bare foot over the morning dew and enjoying the early hours of morning.

I wished him, "Good morning sir"

He replied enthusiastically, "Good morning. How are you young man?"

"I am fine, thanks for asking" I replied as I pulled a chair for myself and sat on it.

 I asked him while pouring a cup of tea for myself, "Would you like to have some tea?"

He walked towards me and said while pulling a chair for him, "Sure".

"Here you go" I said as I prepared a cup for him and placed it on the table in front of him. (By then he got seated comfortably on the chair)

He thanked me and asked while picking up the cup, "What are your plans for today?"

"Nothing special, maybe I would just bask a little" I replied as I moved a little forward to pick up my cup from table.

He took few sips, appreciated the tea and said, "I have been invited by the City College to participate in an orientation program. I am supposed to deliver a lecture there. Would you like to accompany me?

"Are they going to allow me to attend the event? I mean, I am not a student studying in there" I asked curiously.

He said after placing the cup on the table, "Oh, that won't be an issue. I can easily squeeze you in along with my staff."

"In that case, I would surely accompany you to the event" I replied as I picked up the newspaper from the table.

Professor looked at his watch and said, "Its 7:30 am, we need to reach at the venue by 10:00 am"

"I have been to this college before, it's nearby. I don't think it would take us more than 15 minutes to reach there" I said while quickly flipping the pages of newspaper which I had just picked up from the table.

 Thereafter we quickly freshened up, had our breakfast and around 9:30 am we started with our journey to the college.

While driving I asked him, "Professor, what is the topic of your lecture?"

"I have not decided yet, but probably I would highlight the importance of vision and self appreciation, or I might talk about importance of logical analysis of a situation in life. There is a lot to talk about. I will decide it on the spot after assessing the crowd." He replied without looking at me and kept reading and scrolling something on his cell phone.

"Why so?" I asked curiously

He glanced at me and said while looking back at the his mobile screen, "There is no point in sharing if people are not willing to receive it"

He continued and said, "That is why I don't select a specific topic beforehand unless I am attending some conference or seminars having predefined topics or subject."

I was impressed by this simple approach which he had towards the life. He was not at all willing to take any stress of preparation or even performance. It appeared as if he was going to watch a movie or soccer game instead of delivering a lecture in a room full of unfamiliar audience.

He was right when he had said earlier that a well prepared person does not need any last minute preparation. It won't be wrong to accept that knowledge instills confidence.

After driving for couple of more minutes, we reached at the venue where the employees from professor's staff were already present along with the representatives of college administration to receive him.

Professor was right in the sense that no one asked about my credentials once they saw that I was accompanying him. We received a warm welcome and were escorted to the auditorium by the college principal where rest of the college staff and students were waiting for the professor.

After giving a brief but well articulated and impressive introductory speech, the principal handed over the microphone to the professor along with a request to enlighten the young minds. Meanwhile, I was offered a seat by his staff in the first guest row.

Professor took the microphone and walked few steps forward towards the edge of the stage. Now he was standing very close to the students and staff sitting in front row. He waved towards the crowd and said roaring, "Good morning ladies and gentlemen, how are you all today?"

Unexpectedly his greetings generated a warm response, as it appeared to me that the students were addressed differently for the first time. This time, what they heard was new to the ears. They were not addressed as dear students or friends rather professor addressed them as ladies and gentlemen which induced a feeling of maturity and heightened sense of dignity within them.

On listening to his salutation few of the students were seen smiling and some could be seen whispering into each other ears. Whatever may be their expressions or reactions, but one thing was very much clear that the professor was successful in gaining their attention from the very beginning.

He was quick to utilize this momentary attention which his greetings generated for him from the audience; to further hold their attention he immediately hurled a question at them.

He asked, "What do you understand by vision?" He paused for a while and asked further, "have you ever heard about this term 'analysis of a situation'?"

His questions were followed by a pin drop silence. I was impressed by his strategy of acquiring attention of such a huge gathering and that too in a blink of an eye. Amazingly, he was now having their undivided attention.

Now, he started encouraging students to speak up their mind. He was able to instill confidence in them and soon few of the students started coming up with some suggestions and gradually others followed. Within few minutes, his lecture had already transformed into a highly interactive session.

After listening to few of the answers and suggestions he said, "That was a really informative and enlightening session and some of you have come up with really impressive and exceptional ideas."

He continued and said while signaling towards his team sitting in the front row, "I will make sure that the people from my team must note down each and every worthy suggestions and ideas which you all have contributed to. In fact, if your college administration will allow, I would really love to interact with you more often."

This unexpected and unconditional appreciation generated a huge round of applause from the audience. This applause was clear indication of how well he was able to establish a connection with his audience instantly.

Now in order to capitalize on this next leg of enhanced attention, He took few quick steps towards the centre stage and said, "However, coming back to the point. I think, you all will agree with the point that in our day to day life, now and then, we are often challenged by various stressful situations. And in order to manage these situations, we often end up taking advices from family and friends. Unfortunately, most of the times, these advices don't work; leaving us further confused, frustrated, and sometimes even embarrassed.

Have you ever thought why these advices don't work for us, even when they are coming from highly experienced and matured person, sometimes?

No matter how good the advice is and how educated the advisor is, most of the times these advices fail to work, mainly because of:

➢ The inability of the advisor to develop a concord with our mental level,

➢ His inability to understand the emotional turmoil which we are going through and,

➢ To make the things worse he/she often ends up misjudging our capabilities and readiness to execute what that person is advising us to do."

He took few more steps forward and said after sitting on the edge of stage, "Let us try to understand this with the help of a very simple example:

'Suppose there is a high school student, struggling with mathematics. He came to know about a professor who teaches advance mathematics in university and was very popular among his pupil for his innovative teaching ideas and knowledge of the subject.

Somehow, this professor agrees to teach him. Everything looks fine, in fact great in the beginning. However, on the contrary this student still fails to get hold of the concept, even after this newly found assistance in studies.

Can you guess what might have gone wrong in this situation, where we are having a dedicated student being taught by a highly educated person?"

Without waiting for any response he continued and said, "In order to further understand the situation, let's continue with the example;

'After studying for few weeks, this student decided to change the teacher and he was lucky enough to find a neighbour, who happens to be a very popular high school teacher. Amazingly, this time not only his grades improved but now he started understanding the subject better.'

Now pause for a moment and write down your conclusion on a piece of paper, why the student might have failed to perform earlier given the fact that the professor was a highly respected, acclaimed and popular teacher of advanced mathematics, whereas, he succeeded subsequently? (Reader should also try to write down the conclusion in the blank space given below.)

____

____

____

____.

All the parameters appear to be same in both of the circumstances. The student is willing to put in extra efforts and is taught by capable teachers in the both situations. Now, let us try to understand what might have gone wrong here;

☛ *In the first situation,* the professor being habitual of teaching advanced mathematics to his pupil assumed that this student must be having the basic knowledge of the subject and hence he started teaching him accordingly.

We can see that from the very onset, the college professor or we can say the advisor in here was not able to develop a concord with the mental level of the student.

Further, the advisor here also failed to understand the emotional turmoil to which his teachings might have exposed this student, especially when the student repeatedly failed to follow what the professor was teaching him.

Since the college professor, was teaching this student with full dedication, so understandably he was expecting his student to deliver, especially when it was just a high school math. Therefore, he clearly misjudged the abilities and readiness of the student to comprehend and execute what all he was being taught.

Since the advisor here failed to understand the mental level of the student, his emotions and ability to execute what all he was being instructed, therefore the teachings or we can say the advices given were of no use to the recipient or the student in this case.

☞ **Whereas, in second situation** the teacher being a high school teacher was already aware or acquainted with the mental level of the student he was teaching. Since, he knew the mental level of the student therefore somehow he was aware of the capabilities of his student. Hence, he was able to teach him in a manner which proved helpful to the student.

☞ **Now following question might arise in our minds?**

Shall we blame the advisor for failure?

What do you think?

According to me, it won't be fair to blame the advisor.

He is not at fault, because it is not possible for any individual to completely understand the mental level, emotional situation and capabilities of another person accurately. It's simply unrealistic to even expect this from others.

☞ **By now the question that arises in our mind is "What should be done?"**

<u>*What is the solution?*</u>

I have a simple solution for this issue and the solution is:

"We must stop this unending marathon of seeking and accepting advices and opinions. This is your problem and you should try to solve it by yourself. By doing this, you will not only boost up your confidence levels but will also add up to your experience."

☞ **Understand this;**

You are the only one at the receiving end. Therefore, you are expected to know a lot better about the problem than any other person.

Instead of crying out loud on your miseries, brooding and blaming oneself for losses, you should try to stay calm and focus on the problem itself.

> No problem can take you hostage if you are willing to put up a fight.

"Always remember that the problems are not invincible; it is our fear that makes them to appear insurmountable for us".

He walked towards the dais to have some water and then he walked back towards the front stage and continued with his speech and said, "Dear friends, first let me talk about fear. Fear is a disproportionate and extremely emotional response which is often expressed by us towards any unpleasant situation.

Fear is never alone; it is often accompanied by an extended battery of events, which consistently keep running repeatedly in our mind rendering us fearful, useless and unrealistic.

☞ *Let me walk you through the consequences of fear.*

➤ As soon as fear starts gripping us, we panic. We start losing our self confidence and clarity in thoughts resulting in stress.

➤ Our brain and logical thought process succumbs in front of this induced stress, and therefore constructive thoughts stop coming to our mind and instead soon they get replaced by the anxiety and feeling of uncertainty.

➤ In the absence of logical and rational thinking, our ego starts soaring all time high, thereby transforming us into an impulsive, impatient and unreasonable fool.

➤ Finally, we submit to our miseries and accept that we are not efficient and intelligent enough to handle our problem.

In reality by doing this we transform our self into a sitting duck waiting for a helping angel to guide us through.

Soon environment around us starts charging up and people begin noticing our changed body language and behavior.

Now suddenly, everyone starts taking interest in our problem and is eager to play his/her role as a mentor and wants to lead us through.

Even the people struggling in their own lives are eager to guide us through and tell us what to do. Now we are flooded with lot of fresh and stale ideas.

Every human being around you is ready to bail you out. Even a person of subnormal intelligence becomes Einstein for you.

Now you have solutions and lots of them but still you are not able to sort out the issue that you are facing, because often these suggestions doesn't possesses any working credibility.

By seeking other's opinions on your problems, you may or may not be able to find a solution but this surely accredits you with titles like Mr. /Miss confused, tube light or any other synonyms signifying your innate inability to sort out things on your own.

Amazingly, these titles are often bestowed by the same friends, who were eager to advice you earlier.

At the end of day, we are back to square1. Yes of course with added accreditations.

☞ **Have you ever thought what good this habit of seeking suggestions did for us?**

Why have you never asked yourself to not to indulge in this act of clamor which makes you vulnerable to such unrequired and unsolicited ideas and subsequent accreditations?

☞ **My point is very simple and let me put it in this way, if we can trust others then why can't we trust ourselves?**

If we are ready to sit with our friends and colleagues to discuss it over then why we cannot sit with our self and try to figure out what works for us and what not.

If we can listen to their suggestions and ideas, then why can't we listen to our inner voice?

Always remember that the solution lies with in us but we often stray out in search of it.

☛ **Now question arises** *"if solution to our problems lies with in us, then why we are not able to trace it out?"*

In fact, this is one of the most valid questions to ask from oneself, and the answer to this question is very simple.

"The answer is that we have not conditioned our self to do so."

☛ **Before we dive deep further, first let us discuss how most of us often reacts to any unpleasant or challenging situation:**

➤ Whenever we are faced with any problem, the first thing which we do is we panic and get startled.

➤ Soon this influenced state of mind starts affecting our thought process resulting in generation of unrealistic, irrational and negative thoughts which often causes anxiety and further propagates the fear.

➤ Now these irrational and misplaced thoughts start controlling us.

➤ Soon our breathing become shallower, reducing the flow of oxygen to the brain which further leads to the depletion in the efficient functioning of brain hence adversely affect our ability to cope up with stress.

➤ Consequently we start feeling helpless and doomed, as we are unable to think of any possible opportunity or idea to bail us out therefore, the fear of unknown starts gripping us.

➤ At this point of time, we start seeking for any possible help from anyone available but still do not try to look inside us for help.

☞ **Now question arises how can we help our self to resolve such situations?**

⇨ In order to do so we need to develop and work on the following two qualities:

1. Vision

2. The ability to understand and analyze the situation before drawing any conclusions

These two qualities when developed, learned and grasped successfully can turn tables to your side, as both of them insist upon logic and reality.

It won't be an exaggeration to say that these qualities can help us in transforming ourselves into a well- sorted leader rather than a timid joke featuring regularly in the work place gossips.

Now, if these qualities truly inherit so much of power in them, than let us see what they are, what they can help us to achieve, and how they are going to help us?

☞ **The first quality which deserves our attention is "the vision".** *Your vision defines you; it conveys what you are and what you are capable of doing? Vision gives the direction to our life. Our vision not only defines us but it also limits what all we can achieve in our life.*

➤ The vision acts as a template, enabling us to judge right and wrong.

➤ It helps us in careful development and proper execution of plans, with every possible care taken to avoid pitfalls.

➤ Howsoever, if trouble arises, the vision enables us to plan a remedial action therefore vision helps in bailing us out, in the hour of need.

➤ Vision provides face to our imagination, actions to our thoughts and imparts wings to our dreams. It's the driving force which compels us to act.

➤ Your vision distinguishes you from the rest of the crowd. Vision instills confidence in self and in the society. Vision can carve out a leader, a trendsetter out of you.

➤ Vision imparts fuel to the perseverance and makes us to see what lies at the horizon and beyond.

☞ **Now let us discuss how to develop vision?**

➨ First and foremost quality required to develop vision is to learn to have faith in yourself and trust your instincts.

➨ You need to learn to understand the importance of logic and should frequently apply it whenever you have to deal with any situation.

➨ Always remember once you are out of your home everything needs to be logical and practical in life.

➡ Emotions are best suited to be read and described in fictions. Even you need to behave a little practical and logically correct to maintain yours most priced relationships in life.

➡ Learn to always analyze the situation without involving the emotions then only you will be able to see the hidden truth.

☞ *Always remember that it is not a crime to commit mistake, now and then everyone does it. If you have also committed one, simply accept it and put your earnest efforts to sort it out.*

➡ Learn to stand for yourself, never behave like a spineless person and always put up the best possible yet justifiable resistance whenever it is necessary.

➡ Don't let the people override your concerns.

➡ First learn to respect yourself and only then the people will follow.

➡ Try not to hide behind someone, as by doing so you are battering your self confidence, discrediting your reliability and undermining your potentials. Always remember, it is our own actions which often causes severe damages to our self-esteem.

Always remember that we can't go beyond what we can visualize.

☞ **The second quality which deserves our attention is "Understanding a problem and analyzing it".**

This is the most fundamental yet much underrated and unfortunately least implemented practice when it comes to the problem solving.

We often jump to the solution and that too without understanding the problem properly. As a result, we often end up either overreacting or under estimating the problem which we are facing.

We are so obsessed with finding solutions, that we often consider it as an absolute wastage of time to even spare a minute or more to try to thoroughly understand what has actually happened or is happening around us. Let aside thinking about what all possible implications it may have and the repercussions which we might have to face in due course of time?

We never ever care to spare some time to think on these important aspects before reacting.

Due to this obsession of ours for solutions, we act in a haste to arrive at conclusion and consequently end up messing up the situation further.

☞ **Let us try to understand what is happening here?**

We mess up because we are confused. We are confused because in reality we don't know exactly what has happened.

This situation arises mainly because of our habit of jumping to the conclusion, leaving aside several basic but important questions unanswered.

⇨ **Following are some of the very basic and important questions which deserve a very careful and thorough consideration from us, before we jump to any conclusion:**

➤ What has happened?

➤ Why it happened?

➤ How it happened?

➤ Was it preventable?

➤ Do we need to respond at all?

➤ Did we respond appropriately? If not, then what was lagging in our response?

➤ How much serious the situation is?

➤ Would it be possible for us to handle the event/ situation at our own or do we need some sort of expert or professional opinion?

Every question above is significant and has a consequence therefore, these questions needs to be addressed appropriately to enable us to draw a helpful and enabling conclusion.

Let's start discussing these questions in detail.

☞ What has happened and why it happened?

⇨ To begin solving any problem, first and foremost requirement is to know the problem itself and what caused it.

⇨ The answer to this question helps us to understand the basic logic behind the events or incidence which has occurred. The detailed analysis of this question successfully highlights the causes which lead to the ultimate fall out.

⇨ **Irrespective of the fact that whether we are dealing with personal or professional issues, the following sub-questions/ points hold well in each scenario and helps us to trace the root cause of the problem.**

➤ Whether it was an inadvertent error that popped up while working?

➤ Was there any negligence in execution?

➤ Did it happen due to lack of dedication and discipline?

➤ Is it a result of any judgmental error?

➤ Is anyone trying to frame us? Or

➤ Perhaps we were trying to manipulate and lobby against someone else but unfortunately it backfired, leaving us in a mess.

➤ Did we acted or committed under the influence of emotions and are now finding it difficult to fulfill our commitment, or

➤ Are we over accommodative?

(Many times our over accommodative nature causes trouble for us. By indulging in this habit we somehow increase the expectations of the people around us to the extent that they eventually stop caring about our needs as we are always busy putting in our best efforts to meet theirs, thereby leaving us frustrated and dejected.)

➤ Do we trust people blindly?

All of above question are for introspection and not meant to be discussed in public domain.

In majority of the issues which we face in our professional or personal life, some or all of the above factors collaborate and gradually ends up creating trouble for us.

Now by the time when you have successfully answered and analyzed all the sub-questions above, you are clearly able to recognize the exact reason which caused this problem or landed us in the trouble. Now we will move on to the next question for analysis.

☞ Was it preventable?

This question, in itself, talks volumes about our ability to handle and execute competently under stressful situations.

This question calls for a detailed introspection especially if the incidence was preventable.

➤ Like, whether we had some prior but unconfirmed information with us but instead of working on it we decided to overlook.

➤ Whether we had complete information beforehand but were unable to comprehend the facts correctly which eventually lead to the failure?

➤ Whether we had all the information and were well aware of the consequences but failed to act in time, which eventually resulted in the failure?

➤ Whether we had all the information with us, were having time in hand and were aware of the consequences but were afraid to act. So instead of acting we choose to be a mute spectator and allowed it to happen.

The detailed introspection on above points helps us to identify and subsequently work on the factors or habits which prevented us from taking preventive measures beforehand. Now we will walk ahead towards the next question.

☞ **"Our response to a situation"**

⇨ This question allows us to introspect how we react or had reacted under any given circumstance.

⇨ Broadly flight or fight reactions are usually observed whenever we are exposed to stressful circumstances or situations.

➤ Either we would try to run away from the situation or we might even try to hide behind a shield of excuses or looped explanations; or

➤ We would stand our ground and put up a fight in order to defend our interests and values. Instead of shying away, we would accept our mistakes with a genuine intention of rectifying them subsequently.

⇨ In a way, our reaction to any situation is not only expressive of our state of mind but it also talks a lot about our character in general and about our qualities and abilities in particular.

⇨ Therefore, this point deserves a special consideration. This point will act as a template to ponder upon, especially for those who want to eliminate every possible weakness of theirs.

Let us talk about the next question.

☞ **'Do we really need to respond or react at all?"**

This is one of the very important questions in the above list. Often we come across certain innocuous incidences or situations in our day to day life which does not deserve any sort of response from our side.

However, these innocuous events might feel hurtful to our inflated ego. Any response under these situations undisputedly leads to full blown arguments which further add stress to our already stressed life and relationships.

Therefore whenever we encounter such petty situations, we should learn and try to avoid responding whenever it is possible for us. Because no matter how trivial an argument is, it not only consumes our resources like time and energy but also adversely affects our mental health consequently affecting the quality of our work and life.

☞ **Simple trick to master a technique to avoid unnecessary arguments is**: Whenever, you are faced with any trivial issue and you intend to argue about it, just hold back for a second and ask yourself a question – "whether I am willing to pay in terms of my time, energy and mental peace for this issue or incidence?"

If the answer is yes then surely you should go ahead with a heated exchange of words or whatever it takes to win the dispute but if the answer to your question is 'No' then just walk away from that incidence without giving any reaction.

⇨ If in spite of our conscious efforts, we often end up having full blown arguments over trivial matters then it's a high time for introspection. Either you are very emotional person or highly egoist.

⇨ Irrespective of the type of a person who you are, you need to learn to control your emotions and the manner in which these emotions are expressed, because no one can judge you unless you start leaving clues about your personality.

⇨ It's always best to be a little secretive. A little mystery is always helpful in getting people's attention, however, once you have it then it's up to you that how you are going to use this attention to further your interests.

➤ **If you are an emotional person**, it's good for you. Emotions are good, they makes life colorful and worth living until this quality of yours is limited to you or within a very small selected group of trusted people. Because public display of this quality often renders you vulnerable as there are very strong chances that people around you will manipulate you to achieve their objectives and at the end of the day you will feel cheated, rejected and disrespected.

☞ **One of the simplest methods to keep your emotions under check is:-**

Whenever you move out of your comfort space i.e. your home or company of trusted friends to your work place or any other public place you should learn to put up a public face.

Let me simplify this further. Whenever you are in a public life behave professionally leaving no room for emotions or relationships. Nowadays, many companies don't support or encourage deep emotional relationships with office colleagues at work place.

The reason is very simple, once people start interacting emotionally the logic in their conversation or any interaction takes the back seat. Now work is done to please the individual and not with the aim of achieving professional success.

☞ **However, if you are an egoist person** then it won't be bad for you, if you start working on this trait of yours, because it is always better to have high levels of self esteem rather than an ego soaring high.

☞ **One of the simplest methods to keep your ego under check is** to stop over prioritizing yourself. Always remember that excess of everything is bad. Things look good and give perfect results when done in a balanced way. This single effort will yield compounded results for you.

Therefore, whenever you are in public place stay in your expected role. If you are an entrepreneur; act, think and behave like one.

If you are a working professional then your demeanors must speak aloud about your professional competence, dedication and professionalism.

Once you have successfully learnt to carry yourself professionally at your work place then possibility of emotional outbursts at work place reduces significantly, making your life much easier and richer.

Now let us talk about the next question.

☞ **"The adequacy of response"**

This is one of the most important and deciding aspect of any interaction that we have.

☞ **On professional grounds**: -

➤ The adequacy of response is directly related to the chances of success.

➤ Any inadequate response given from our side is often perceived as sign of incompetence and carelessness by the employer and it consequently predisposes us to anxiety, nervousness and the feeling of underperformance.

> Whereas over response not only leads to the divulging of unnecessary details to the recipient but also makes us to look like a bragging and overconfident person, certainly this is not a good image to have in your workplace.

☞ **On personal grounds**: -

> The adequacy of response is directly related to the warmth, comfort and mental peace which we are going to enjoy in our relationships.

> Under response from your end can make the other person, depending upon his/ her state of mind or mental makeup, feel unimportant, ignored or even dejected.

> Whereas, any over response or over reaction often leads to unpleasant arguments and feelings of resentment which if not addressed suitably often proves detrimental to the healthy relationships.

Therefore, it is in our best interest to assess the situation properly before giving a befitting reply. Let's talk about our next question in line.

☞ **How much serious the situation is?**

➤ Whenever we are in a situation we often focus more on it's momentarily aspects, hence channelizing most of our energy and resources in sorting out the issue to get an interim or immediate relief.

➤ However, we tend to overlook the long term consequences which it might have on us.

➤ Therefore, it is always better to do a quick analysis of the situation before tackling it. Especially, if it involves any financial aspect, intimidating circumstances or any other situation which might possibly affect your carrier or personal life in long run.

It is well said that it's better to be safe than sorry.

Let us talk about the next question

☞ **Would it be possible for us to handle the event/ situation at our own or do we need some sort of expert or professional opinion?**

This aspect of any problem must not be overlooked under any circumstances.

There are several situations both in personal and professional life which require interventions at different stages. We all know this but still hesitate to ask for help. Have you ever thought why it is so?

There are many attributing factor which develops this feeling of hesitancy towards seeking help. Some of important contributing factors are

➤ **Hidden fears**: those unexplained fears, which prevent us from leading a normal life. We are aware of them but can't do anything about them.

There is a long list of phobias which can be downloaded from the internet, which implies that it is perfectly normal to have hidden fears as most of us do have one or another type of fear.

Since, it is a common occurrence to have fear, therefore there is nothing wrong or shameful in accepting your fears in front of others but in a dignified way.

This simple declaration gives you confidence and now you can very easily stay out of the harm way as people around you will neither force you and nor will judge you, provided you exhibits adequate confidence while accepting your fears and not showcasing them as your limitations for which you seek sympathies from others.

➤ **Mistrust in system** – based on other people's opinions we also fall prey to this misconception that systems don't work, they are just to harass and fool people but it's not true.

A society is as good as its systems are. Therefore, instead of making illusory assumptions it is far better to check the truth by our own experience. Systems are in place to help common people and they are working day and night for us.

In fact, it is the propaganda of the unruly elements to malign the image of the systems so that people should refrain from seeking redressal hence end up giving them a free passage.

➤ **Lack of self-confidence** – this also plays a vital role, especially in the hours of need. Because when we are not so confident about our own self, we tend to indulge in the practice of fault finding and we don't stop until we are able to find one or more reason which might hold us responsible for whatever bad has happened.

By finding these reasons we pacify ourselves thereby losing the last possible chance of self improvement.

➤ **Emotional blackmailing and Social stigmas:**

Both of the above reasons also play a very significant role in limiting our access to the redressal.

However; we need to understand that it's our life, our individual identity which is being targeted or is under threat and therefore the situation needs to be addressed suitably and on priority.

Societies and emotions will exist only when we exist, they have no meaning or even existence without us in it. So there is no logic in giving preference to emotions or society over and above our own well being and safety.

Just focus on your personal improvement and wellbeing because any improvement in your life is directly as well as indirectly going to affect the quality of your life as well as that of the people around you.

Moreover, no one needs such relationships or people who cannot come for our rescue in the hour of need.

Therefore, whenever the situation calls we should be able to openly seek help and expert opinions for safe guarding our life and interests."

Now we can clearly appreciate that, there are so many different aspects to a problem that we often ignore, the aspects which are in fact instrumental in understanding and analyzing the problem which we are facing. (We need to understand and analyze a situation before embarking on our quest to find the appropriate solution.)

Spending few minutes in analyzing and understanding the situation not only increases our awareness of the circumstances but it also increases our possibility of arriving at some working solution.

Unfortunately, in reality as a matter of habit, whenever we are faced with any problem or situation we only focus on one fact and that fact is, "we are in trouble and god knows what will happen to us now".

This tendency of ignoring the analysis part of the problem solving invariably induces fear, anxiety, a feeling of uncertainty and above all makes our life miserable.

☛ **Now I will discuss about the most interesting but detrimental part of our problem solving practice**.

We our self don't know properly what the situation is or what exactly has gone wrong with us? But still we immediately start responding or begin seeking advices from other.

Since, the people from whom we seek advices or suggestions have often not witnessed the event or situation personally; therefore, they solely rely upon us for the input regarding the distressing event/ situation for which we are seeking their advice.

Since we have not allowed our self with the necessary time required for analyzing and understanding the situation, we our self don't have more than 60% of the understanding of the event, sometimes this percentage is even lesser.

Now, with limited understanding of the situation when we try to explain it to another person and that too in a panicked state, we often miss out on several minute details which either was considered unnecessary by us or we have failed to notice them at all.

So eventually we are able to transmit only 30 to 40% of the relevant information to the person from whom we are seeking advice or suggestion.

Now depending upon his/her caliber, state of mind, extent of concern towards us, his/her own nature and the amount of time that person could spare to listen to us; he/ she is able to understand 15 to 30% of our situation.

The craziest part is that our response to the situation is often guided by the person who is having even less than 30% knowledge or understanding of the issue.

That's why when we acts on the given advices, blindly, they fail to address the root cause of the problem and hence the efforts which we put in often goes down the drain leaving us further distressed and infuriated.

⇨ **Let us analyze the above situation of problem solving and try to break it further for better understanding of the concept:**

In order to analyze the above situation of problem solving, we need to break it into 2 situations or parts.

In first part we will try to understand the chain of events when we attempt to solve a problem without analyzing and understanding it properly.

Whereas in the second part, we will get to know how the same situation becomes completely different when we attempt solving the same problem but after taking our time to analyze and understand it properly before making any attempt to solve it personally or with the help of someone else.

⇨ **Part-I: Solving problems without analyzing them:-**

Case-I: Information with you (without bothering to analyze the situation) is not more than 60% of what has happened.

Since every problem needs some sort of redressal, so we are bound to respond. We have two options with us, either we can act on our own or in case we are unable to find any appropriate answers on our own, we often decide to seek someone else advice on this situation.

Let us try to explore both of our options with the help of illustrations below:

a) Seeking advice from the other person:-

 Information with person who is giving you advice is less than 30% of what has happened, mainly because the person has not himself witnessed the event so he is completely dependent on us for the all relevant inputs.

But with limited understanding of the situation we can't help him much.

When we panic or are in a stressful situation, it is quite natural and possible for anyone to skip the sequence of events or even some of the details which might appear less important and less significant to us.

So while sharing our limited information with other person, it is quite possible for us to omit out those less significant appearing details from the account of the event, which we are going to share with the other person, from whom we are seeking an advice.

Now it is perhaps very difficult for that person to give us a very useful advice especially when he has access to only limited information. Hence, quite often such advices do not work for us especially in the way expected by us.

b) Acting on our own: any action taken or response given in haste is often flawed. However, when we are faced with pressing situations we cannot wait indefinitely, we need to act and sometimes we need to act promptly.

The biggest problem with lack of information is that the voids created by it are often filled up by the emotions.

The emotions like fear and anxiety are the first to follow. Once invoked, these emotions don't sit idle they start raking up our mind with all sort of unnecessary thoughts, speculations and annoying memories which should have been forgotten long ago.

As of result of this, another member in the form of apprehension jumps in to join this bandwagon of emotions meant for unsettling our mind.

Now we don't only have the limited knowledge of the situation but are also having an unsettled and apprehensive mind which is full of fear and anxiety.

Now there is nothing much left to speculate how we are going to react in the above situation. It will certainly be a disaster.

There is a considerable chance that instead of doing goods for us, it might inflict further damage.

Therefore, it is always recommended to avoid responding in the heat of the moment instead take few moments to first understand the situation and then act suitably.

⇨**<u>Part-II: Solving problems after thorough analysis:</u>**

Case - II: Information with you after understanding and analyzing the situation thoroughly before making any conclusion is more than 90% of what has happened.

The habit of thoroughly analyzing a situation before responding gives us a fair chance to clearly figure out the matter.

It allows us to ask certain questions from ourselves and people around us so that we are able to understand better what has happened and why it happened? Could we have prevented it from happening? Is there any possibility of recurrence?

This habit of analyzing also happens to buy us a little extra time to think with cool head and then come out with a fool proof action plan.

We can think about all sorts of situations or question such as:

➤ In first place, do I need to respond at all?

➤ Is the situation worth responding? If yes, then how should we approach and what should be the intensity of our response.

➤ Is there any possibility of further damage? If so, then is it possible for us to prevent that damage?

➤ Will there be any repercussions of our actions, if so, then how are we going to counter it?

➤ What might be the best way to resolve the issue? Are we over thinking or over reacting to the situation?

When we are through with this process of analyzing of the situation we have the complete picture of the situation in our hands and we already know how we are going to handle the current situation/ crisis or event.

Even if we ought to seek someone's help we will be better able to share credible and relevant information with that person from whom we are seeking an advice or help.

It is very much clear from above analysis that chance of getting an efficient and appropriate working solution is far better in situation (II).

Professor walked few steps forward on the stage and asked, "Don't you think it would be much easier for you to solve your problem if you know more than 90% of it?"

His question generated a huge response and students responded with a loud "yes" as an answer.

He smiled and continued with his speech and said further, Dear friends, "Now we know that the proper understanding of situation is indispensable in problem solving".

He walked back towards the dais and said, "There is an old saying that "the eyes will see, only if brain knows".

Understanding a problem means knowing the problem. This simple act of comprehending a problem automatically makes us understand the following important aspects of any situation:

☛ What is the real cause underlying the problem, and how to address it?

☛ Whether the problem is psychological or work related?

☛ Do problem really exist or it's just an apprehension?

When you have done with answering all of the above questions, you will feel a limited need for seeking any help or opinion from anyone else, unless you are looking for any medical, legal or any other professional assistance.

Let us discuss what all difference this habit of analyzing can make in one's life:

➤ To begin with, simply by trying to understand the problem you are well into it and unknowingly have already started fixing it and that too with out any assistance or guidance.

➤ Soon you will realize that you are no more a confused person as now you know precisely what you are looking at and you know exactly what you want to do and how to do it.

➤ Now you are no more an energy sucker but a much-sorted after think-tank. It may sound a little exaggerating and surprising but shortly the same people who were earlier in your advisory council will come looking for an advice.

➤ Every impossible is made possible simply by sorting out, one by one, every possible aspect out of the impossible and soon you are done with it.

➤ Just follow your vision, understand and analyze the situation as closely as possible. Soon you will be having all the necessary answers with you.

Problems do speak for themselves, you just have to learn to reach out and hear them out."

That will be all for today. Dear friends, I must thank you all for listening to me with such an admiring patience and exceptional attention and participation.

 I hope that all of you brilliant and smart, men and women will try to implement in your life what all you have learnt today.

With this note, I end my lecture. Thanks for listening to me. Bye", he placed his mike on dais and walked back towards his chair.

He got standing ovation from the students, teachers and everyone who listened to his spell bounding inspiring words.

Till that day, I haven't realized that lectures could sound such lively, meaningful and crisp. In fact, his lecture felt like a breeze to me, it was over before you could realize it.

After the speech, we attended the lunch that was hosted by the college administration to honor the professor.

It was a mesmerizing experience. The event was over by 3pm. I complemented him for his performance and headed towards our car.

To express my respect for him, I took few quick steps ahead of him and swiftly opened the car door for him. He looked a little astonished;

he thanked me and hopped inside the car. I too got inside the car and we started with our journey back.

On our way back to home, we happened to stop at a red-light for a while. Before, we could drive past, the professor said while looking out of the window, "Son, if it's ok with you, I would like to catch some breath"

He looked at me and said while pointing towards the park, "Would you like to come along?"

"Sure, why not." I turned on the indicator and maneuvered the car slowly towards the side of the road and then took the first exit out of the main road to the service lane and parked the car on one of the designated parking slots.

We entered the park; it was a well maintained park. After walking for a while we decided to sit under a big banyan tree. I was a little hesitant to sit on a somewhat muddy tree seat but it was not an issue for the professor.

He quickly selected a comfortable looking spot under the shade of the tree and sat comfortably on it with his back resting against the stem of tree.

The professor was looking very calm and composed, by looking at him no one can believe that, this man had just delivered a mind- blowing lecture and has accrued an overwhelming appreciation and recognition to his credit. To me he looked like a saint, a yogi untouched by the worldly accolades and appreciations.

Unable to hide by inquisitiveness I said, "Professor, can I ask you something?"

"Please go ahead" He replied calmly.

"I just want to know how people's response does not affect you. Earlier in the day when we had entered the auditorium, in fact no one appeared willing to listen to you, I noticed that you were not at all nervous and after delivering such a phenomenal speech neither are you elated by receiving such a huge round of applause and appreciation." I asked while looking inquisitively towards him

After listening to my question he smiled and said, "I must admit you are a keen observer."

I asked instantly, "Sir, please tell me how do you manage to do this?"

Without waiting for his reply I continued bombarding him with my subsequent question and asked, "I want to know the secret behind this ability of yours? Hope you won't mind sharing it with me?"

Professor shifted a little to sit in an upright position and replied after sitting in an upright position, with his hands placed comfortably on his knees, "I was expecting this question. What you have observed is right, my peace of mind is not subjected to suggestions, neither do I feel elated by any appreciation nor do I become depressed on listening to criticism".

He glanced at me and said while looking at the people walking by, "I firmly believe in the fact that, I am the only one, who knows better about my own capabilities, responsibilities, circumstances, limitations and resources; so how can any another person, who is completely unaware of the songs and sorrows of my life can predict or judge anything about me as accurate and as precise as I can do it myself.

I believe in self-appreciation and logical analysis of the situation before arriving at any conclusion. My ears are deaf to those who criticize me out of jealousy and to those who appreciate me in order to fulfill their manipulative vices."

After completing this statement professor reclined on the trunk of the tree and said smilingly, "Son, if you want to ask something else, go ahead. I will answer it to the best of my knowledge."

Initially, I was a bit reluctant to ask further, however his question instilled a confidence in me, so I said, "Sir, would you like to explain, what do you mean by self-appreciation and how can it help me?" ....and I would like to know about the logical analysis of the situation too.

Professor said interrupting, "Not so fast son, these concepts are not some bed time stories meant to amaze and entertain; these are hard forged experiences of life, so listen to them carefully, one by one, and try to implement them in your day to day routine to ascertain about their usefulness and then you can utilize these concepts for betterment of your life."

He continued, "First we will talk about self - appreciation".

....✳ ✳ ✳...

What to do?

Whenever you are stuck in a loop and are not able to come out with any workable solution for your problems or any situation, try to investigate your problem with the help of following fact assessment sheet.

⇨ **Fact Assessment Sheet**

Sl. No	Issue	Your reply
1.	What has happened?	
2.	Why it happened?	
	➤ Whether it was an inadvertent error?	
	➤ Was there any negligence in execution?	
	➤ Was there any indiscipline?	
	➤ Was it a judgment failure?	
	➤ Is anyone trying to frame me Or my manipulation backfired against me?	
	➤ Did I act under the influence of emotions or substance?	
	➤ Am I over accommodative?	
	➤ Did I trust people blindly?	
3.	Was it preventable, if yes then how?	
	➤ I overlooked the issue.	
	➤ I failed to comprehend the issue or situation correctly.	

	➤ I failed to provide timely intervention.	
	➤ I was afraid to act.	
4.	Do I need to respond at all?	
5.	Was my response appropriate and adequate if not, then what was lacking in it?	
6.	How much serious the situation is?	
7.	Do I need any assistance?	

Now make your objective assessment and write your neutral conclusion below and you could easily see for yourself how much better understanding of the situation you do have now.

____

____

____

____

____

____

____

____

Chapter-6

(Self-appreciation & the Concept of 5min Analysis)

"What we feel about our self is more important than what others think about us"

Professor continued and said, "Self-appreciation is the act of acknowledging your own achievements and praising your own efforts.

We work to get recognition, fame and acknowledgement. We work hard and are willing to exert even harder just to ensure that at the end of day we get money and appreciation for whatever good work we have accomplished.

Believe it or not, words of appreciation has got such immense power in them, once we hear them, our body forgets all the pain and mind is relieved of all the tensions.

No matter how tired we are, few words of genuine appreciation are enough to spread a spontaneous smile across our face.

The work appears to be worth doing and all the efforts well done.

Now question arise; **what if no one is around to appreciate our work?**

How should we feel if, people around us are not wise enough to appreciate the work?

In addition, there may be people around you who are not willing to appreciate you. They may have their valid reasons for doing so, such as jealousy, rivalry or any other ulterior motives which are strong enough to blind their wisdom.

Such people will not appreciate anything good done or achieved by you; rather they will put in their best to pull you down. We are very often faced with such people and circumstances.

"Then what should we do?"

If no one is appreciating us, should we stop doing work, as there is no reward or appreciation for whatever good we are doing or has done?

If people are having malicious tendencies and are just not happy and willing to accept your efforts and success then what would you do?

What do you think what should be done? (The readers should write their opinion on the space below:

____

____

____

____

____

⇨ **In absence of any external motivation and appreciation;**

➤ Should we feel sad and sorry for our self as no one is appreciating us in spite of our good work? And instead of appreciating us, people are involved in nitpicking and are not leaving a stone unturned in order to undermine our success and to condemn us

Or

➢ We should feel proud of whatever good we have achieved, no matter how small or big the achievement is we should be able to say enthusiastically to our self;

Yes, I have done it!

☞ **Let me tell you why I emphasize so much on self appreciation;**

We need to understand few points very clearly and precisely, and they are,

➢ When no one bothers to advice us, help us earnestly when we are down with our failures or are struggling day and night to accomplish our task, then why should we care for their opinions at the end of show.

➢ When, we have faced the wrath of circumstances and toiled hard to accomplish our task then I feel that we and only we have the right to evaluate our performance at emotional level to know whether we succeeded or failed in our pursuit.

➢ You should learn to appreciate your self because only you know how hard you have exerted and how important the task was.

➢ Do not let the spoilers steal away your success.

➢ This is your success and you should learn to acknowledge and reward it.

➢ Allow your inner voice to praise you, emotions are real when you can feel them from the core of your heart; imagine how much real and rewarding the appreciation would feel especially when it is directly coming from your heart.

➤ The smile which spontaneously spreads out wide on our face when we achieve something is the appreciation that our soul showers on us, our heart starts pounding and clapping in rejoice and body become youthful and rejuvenated, it is the most satisfying and the divine appreciation that one can get and should often look for.

➤ What we feel about our self is more important than what others think about us.

➤ We need a constant feedback to stay motivated by reminding our self of our targets, by appreciating and acknowledging the every single possible effort that we have put in to achieve those targets and by cherishing our success.

➤ This will not only improve our efficiency but it will also add a lot to our confidence and will help us in staying motivated.

➤ This transformation in self will eventually be reflected as an overall improvement in our performance.

☞ Now question arises, **"If self appreciation is so much important than how to do it"?**

⇨ First and foremost, you will have to learn to trust yourself;

➤ When you will start to trust yourself then only you will be able to develop an acceptance towards your own opinions and thoughts.

➤ When you have developed an acceptance towards your thoughts, every opinion of yours will count.

➤ Most importantly you will be able to believe in, cherish and applaud the words, which you have said or are going to say to yourself, making the whole act of self-appreciation possible and fruitful.

⇨ Secondly, you need to have a well- developed vision, which will enable you to differentiate between right and wrong, true and phony.

➤ The vision helps in establishing the validity of your opinion and thoughts on the canvas of reality.

⇨ Finally, always remember that you are the only one who knows the true value of your efforts and your own worth, so do not let others opinion about you override your interests.

➤ People around you are themselves surrounded by a lot of problems and miseries just like you do, so their thoughts and opinions are bound to carry some amount of bias, discrimination, ego and sometimes even negativity.

➤ More over you are just another person to them, so you might not get the necessary importance and attention that you deserve.

➤ Lastly, I cannot find a single reason which might convince me to add importance to the appreciation done by people surrounding us.

The people around you and their words of appreciation are just like winds, which can flow in any direction. If you are strong enough to create pressure gradient, they will start flowing towards you.

It does not matter whether you treat yourself or give yourself incentives in order to acknowledge your achievements or not. What matters the most is the feeling that you get from the core of your heart for doing something remarkable, or having achieved something that others failed to achieve, or having accomplished the task which you have assigned to yourself and that too within stipulated time.

This feeling of accomplishment, glory, success, content and proud itself prompts you to perform better and better in future.

There is nothing strong and determined than the self-guided will to perform and succeed".

Professor asked as he looked towards me, "is there anything which you want me to repeat or something that you were not able to get hold off."

His words were lucid, precise and mostly self-explanatory. Whatever he told me was genuinely agreeable and neither was I having any objection against what he had told me.

Therefore, after thinking for a while I replied, "Professor, I do not have any doubts regarding the content of your lecture neither do I disagree with your point of view. But, what I want to know is how to develop faith in self, because as per your lecture faith in self and vision is the key to self-appreciation. You have already enlightened me regarding vision, now I want to know about faith."

He was looking at the children playing next to us. After listening to my question he turned towards me and said, "This is what I like best about you. I am impressed by your ability to listen carefully, comprehend accurately and ask precise questions. This saves time."

He said while again shifting his gaze back on to the children playing near us, "Now coming back to your question, "How to develop faith in self?"

Before he could begin with the topic I asked him interrupting, "Professor if you don't mind me asking, please tell me why your lecture is often a monologue?"

Professor smiled a little and said, "Because I prefer to maintain the continuity of the words. Always remember, words are far dangerous than any weapons invented by man. So it is wise to handle them carefully, especially when you are teaching or guiding someone.

The person receiving education from you is going to follow you and your words by the letter and spirit. Therefore, I prefer a monologue so that the message is conveyed with proper perspective and without any distortion or deviation."

Now professor was about to start with new topic and that was:

"Faith and how to develop it in self"

Although, I have heard a million of times regarding the topics which he was talking about but once he starts narrating, everything appears to be new and different.

....❀ ❀ ❀...

137

What to do?

5 <u>minute analysis</u>

Develop a habit of doing self analysis at the end of every working day.

Last five minutes, before leaving your desk must be dedicated to this purpose. Even, if you are doing a late sitting or overtime, then also invariably dedicate the last 5 minutes of the working day for this task.

During this time, you should take out your pen and dairy, and note down following details for objective analysis of your day's work:

Sl. No.	Event	Outcome	Your resolution
	What has happened?	What it resulted in?	What you should have done/ are going to do to overcome it.

This 5 min exercise will enable you to better analyze and comprehend the situations at work. Whatever the situation might be, this 5min analysis will help you to properly dissect and understand the issue peacefully.

Once you are done with this 5min analysis you will be able to leave the office much centered and that too without any stress; because now you have a clearer picture of the events in your mind and you are already prepared accordingly to handle it next morning.

However, care must be taken while doing this analysis as it is not a tool for self bashing or self criticism.

This must be treated as an enabling tool and not a device meant for demeaning or demoralizing one selves. Principles of logical analysis of a situation must be kept in mind while doing this 5 min analysis.

This habit will enable you to lead a quality personal life as you won't be mixing your professional life with your personal life.

Immediately after the working hours are over, we all have this tendency of running to home or wherever we prefer to be after work, and there is nothing abnormal or new in it.

In fact, this habit of ours in nothing but few of the remaining vestiges of our childhood, when we all used to rush out of the classroom as soon as the last bell rang. But now circumstance have changed a lot

Now when we leave office without giving ourselves the time and opportunity to analyze what has happened at work, we practically take those issues and thoughts along with us to whatever place we are going.

No matter whether we are at home, club or gym, we repeatedly keep on thinking about the events of the day. This leads to mental stress which adversely affects our health as well as our personal life.

When we leave our work place after doing this 5 min analysis, we are not only able to ascertain our shortcomings properly but are also able to think of a suitable resolution/ redressal before we leave our work place.

Now no matter whether we head towards our home, club or wherever we want to go, we will go as a happy and free soul, without carrying any burden or stress of the work along with us.

Chapter-7

(How to Develop Faith in Self & the Concept of Golden Triad)

"If you can trust yourself than only others are going to trust you."

The most miraculous word in English literature is faith. Faith provides strength to our thoughts, conviction in actions and certainty in execution. Having faith helps us in leading a much fuller, happier and productive life.

Faith in itself is the key to perseverance, because when we trust something firmly then we do not yield easily to failures.

We all will accept to the fact that the projects or activities, which we truly believe in gets accomplished more easily and that too in a limited time rather than those activities in which we do not believe in or which are forced on us.

☞ **Now question arises, why it is so***?*

> As in both circumstances the worker, environment, timings, team members and everything else is same but output is drastically different. Why so?

⇨ **Answer is very simple,**

> When we trust anything, (be it a person, place or an event) doubts fade away, thus giving us the exact picture of what is required and how it will be accomplished.

This certainty in execution relieves our mind of the undue stresses and a relaxed mind is always more focused and hence more productive.

It is our faith in god, which make us to look up to him for inspiration, for blessings and for our well being.

Surprisingly, we feel strong and rejuvenated in return as our faith in god assures us that he would take care of us, no matter how hard the situation is and often we start afresh with full potential and doubled the efforts.

If having faith in god can bring so much change, then imagine how much better life we can lead just by simply having faith in self.

☞ **"How to develop faith in self"?**

This is a very simple exercise, all we have to do is:

⇨ **Talk to yourself; ask plenty of questions from your self; like**

> ➤ Why I failed to deliver?
>
> ➤ What went wrong?
>
> ➤ Is my working style wrong?
>
> ➤ Do I lack in a particular skill?
>
> ➤ Are my emotions affecting my work?
>
> ➤ Am I not able to impress others?

If you are not able to impress others, ask following questions from yourself:

> ➤ Is my dressing inappropriate?

> ➤ Am I not good with words?

> ➤ Is something wrong with my body language?

> ➤ Any other question which comes to your mind and you consider it relevant then go ahead and answer it.

Keep on probing yourself with a lot of questions until you run out of them and then put in your best efforts to sort out honest and logical answers to each of the questions that you have asked from yourself.

Remember that nothing happens without a reason and if you are failing, it ought to have been associated with an underlying cause; it's better to find and sort it out before others do the honor by embarrassing you.

These answers, which you will get after probing yourself, will clear your doubts regarding your efficiency and capabilities. Now you are having a list of flaws which need to be corrected to achieve desired goals in life.

Since you are now well aware of your capabilities and limitations, it makes you less vulnerable to manipulations and suggestions.

More you come to know about yourself better you become, gradually everything around you starts falling in line. From your decision making to communication, from planning to execution each and every aspect of your personal and professional life improves considerably.

When you know exactly about your strengths and weaknesses then you automatically learn to say, "No" to the people; especially when according to you their demands or expectations are irrational, overtaxing or inappropriate.

Only a person who knows exactly what he is capable of doing and what not, can say, "NO" to the people offering him something that he finds to be beyond his capability and expertise level.

Always remember you need to have self-confidence and better knowledge to refuse rather than to accept an offer.

You can only say no when you know your limitations. It is far better to accept your limitations and say no to others rather than to fell short of the task due to your inefficiency.

When you have noted down answers to all of the questions then you should sit down and start analyzing your answers with a stable state of mind.

Always remember, whenever you are doing a self analysis for any purpose, you must do it as a third person and put in your best efforts to catch your shortcomings honestly and bravely.

We should always keep in mind one golden rule of self - analysis and that is

"The analysis must be done impartially and emotions must be kept aside while doing analysis".

Because any emotional approach in this context will compromise the entire exercise as you might start criticizing yourself instead of introspection, which will inevitably lead to the failure of this entire exercise.

Purpose of this exercise is to trace and eliminate weaknesses from our self. We are not doing this to highlight our weaknesses and then start cursing our self for possessing them and further adding miseries to our life.

> We are doing this exercise because we intend to find out our mistakes, work on them and correct them, before these mistakes may become the cause of embarrassment or loss in future.

These mistakes, when rectified in time will improve our performance, confidence and efficiency, thereby improving our overall quality of life.

(With these words, he ended his lecture. Like always, his explanations were simple, precise and lucid. His flawless words, depth of knowledge, vast experience and confident body language makes him an exceptional orator.

 He spoke with such a remarkable conviction that I instantly wanted to believe in whatever he had spoken about. Truly, he was the master of his words.)

After a brief pause, he said as he glanced at his watch, "Young man, I think we have spent a lot of time here. We should make our move towards home now"

"Yes, it is getting dark" I replied as we got up and started walking towards the car parking. His narration was so engrossing that I completely lost the track of time. However, his advices were worth listening and helpful too.

We walked towards car and I opened the door for him, he thanked me with a smile and we started with our journey back to home.

While I was driving, he was asking a lot of questions about my work and the people working with me. I was a bit reluctant to share my work place problems with him. After all I was not willing to look like an idiot or a loser in front of him. So, I tried my best to ward off any of the intrusive or more details oriented questions.

Being a wise person he judged my situation much faster than I had expected and then all of sudden, he started telling me about his experiences in previous universities, which was quite interesting to listen.

He said, "Many years ago, when I was not as popular as now, I used to teach human psychology in a college. I used to put my heart and soul in my lectures. Soon, I started gaining popularity among students and this annoyed some of the staff members including the vice-principal.

Within a month time, our college staff got divided into groups and obviously, I was in the crosshairs. Now they were gossiping and hatching new conspiracies against me every day. This was making me furious and agitated and soon my restlessness started showing in my professional and personal life.

Gradually my performance started to decline, often I started losing my temper in classes and would scold my students sometimes even without any strong reasons. This was something which I had never done before.

Now instead of sitting in library and preparing for my lecture, I would sit in cafeteria and would discuss with my group and friends the new strategy to counter the other group.

I indulged in all sort of practices from wooing the principal by inviting him over dinner and complaining about other teachers, to setting toughest examination papers, so that I should have more impact on students than rest of the staff.

Soon in college, I was into the mind games instead of teaching. Most of my working hours were consumed by this ongoing tussle of power and influence and when I used to reach home, I always felt exhausted, fatigued, irritable and impulsive.

It appeared to my wife that I was running out of the emotions and feelings for her. But that was not true. I always loved her but had forgotten my ways to express it to her.

She was right at large; this protracted work place politics had started showing its effects on me. Gradually, I had started to nag her for everything; whatever she would say I would always come up with some brainy solution spoiling her mood and feelings.

Soon, I started criticizing her for her uncooperative and non-understanding behavior. She had said once or twice that I have changed a lot but her statement seemed illogical to my so called highly educated and logical mind.

Unable to bear my behavior any further, finally she decided to leave me. When she announced her decision I was shocked and instead of trying to patch the things up I again scolded her for her unsympathetic attitude towards me. After listening to my unmindful statements she said, "I am going to stay at my parents home, if you are able to find out what went wrong in-between us then rectify it and take me back, else I will send you divorce papers, just sign and send them back to me".

She left and next morning when I reached college, students were demonstrating against me. This was shocking as the students were protesting against their one of the most favorite and loved teacher. I was in the eye of storm; everything was getting worse for me, both at my work place and at home.

(Professor stopped for a while, took out a cigar from his coat pocket and lighted it. He took few puffs while looking straight into the dark road that we were traversing. Taken aback by his account I started wondering, if this was his past then how he had transformed himself into such a successful man.)

I applied the brakes and pulled over the car and asked him, "Are you all right professor?"

Surprisingly, professor smiled and patted on my shoulder and said, "Please don't stop, keep driving otherwise we will be late for dinner." So I continued driving towards home.

Professor puffed his cigar and said, "These events came as a shock for me. I had always loved my wife from the core of my heart and teaching was the only significant dream that I ever had, and I was shocked to see both of them moving out of my life, together.

I was not willing to lose any of them at any cost, so I decided to introspect. I spent days altogether thinking and analyzing. I took an official leave for a full month, avoided answering phone calls for weeks together and kept introspecting till I was able to get hold of the situation.

Gradually, my efforts started showing some positive results and I started getting answers to my questions. Finally, I was able to trace the golden triad of problems".

He paused for a while and asked while looking at me, "are you familiar with the concept of **'the golden triad of problem'**?"

"No, I am not. What is it?" I replied little hesitantly

Professor said, "Whenever anything happens with us or we are faced with any demanding situation, we should try to calm down and focus our self to find answers to the golden triad of problem."

He continued and said, "The golden triad consists of three important questions, which are;

➤ **What has happened?**

➤ **How it happened? And**

➤ **Why it happened?**

Although, in first go these questions appears to be quite simple and easy to answer. However, it is not like that; these questions are not as simple as they appear to us. Because in order to reach at any working and useful solution, we need to answer all of these questions in an unbiased, realistic and logical way.

This can only be achieved with the help of a relaxed and composed state of mind, because a relaxed state of mind not only improves our judgment but is also helps to rule out any possibility of bias.

Therefore, in order to successfully answer these questions of the golden triad, I practiced and developed qualities like:

➤ **Stop brooding,**

➤ **Learn to manage my thinking process,**

➤ **Start analyzing the situations logically,**

⇨ In addition to above, I put in all my efforts to learn traits like:

➤ **Avoid seeking sympathies from people,**

➤ **Never, take the situations personally,**

➤ **Never be emotionally driven,**

➤ **Never, hesitate to accept your failure.**

As a result of this thorough introspection, now I was a changed man. My transformation surprised everyone at college.

Once again I became the most popular teacher in college, although the opposition existed but it become invisible to my eyes.

Most importantly, I got my wife back in my life, and she was happy too. Since that day, she never ever complained of anything again. She was extremely happy and emotional to see this transformed version of mine. This is the biggest achievement of my life.

His account moved me but I was happy to know that his story had a happy- ending.

He looked at me, patted gently on my shoulder and said, "I am noticing you from the day we had met and I can say with certainty that you are pure from heart. Don't worry; I know you are born to win, just learn to trust your instincts and follow them".

I was not able to understand the relevance of his statement at this point of time, in mean time we were about to reach home, so I said wittily, "look professor we are on time and you won't miss your dinner."

Professor laughed loudly and said, "Thank you young man, I am really hungry now."

We entered the home; had our dinner, as it was a long hectic day so there were no more after dinner conversations.

I was lying on my bed, unable to sleep; his story was flashing through my mind repeatedly. Soon, I started comparing his story with my life, and surprisingly a lot of similarities were there.

Except for the facts that he was married, where as I have a girl friend, he was a teacher and I am an executive, rest almost everything was same. If we make these few changes in it, then it surely become the story of my life, this profound similarity made me wonder, whether his principles can help me too? Lost in the thoughts soon I fell asleep.

....❋❋❋..

What to do?

Stage–I: Working on your self

Make a chart and fill in all the answers honestly under the column present status and then start working on your short comings which had lead to the failure and revisit the chart after a week's time to log your progress under the column of reviewed status.

This chart will help you to keep track of the progress. Keep on repeating the process after next 7 days till you are able to overcome the short comings which had lead you to the failure. Once you have successfully addressed your shortcomings then make a final entry under the column final resolution.

Then we will move on to the next stage, i.e. stage-II

Sl. No.	Question	Present Status	Reviewed status after 7 days	Final resolution
1	Why I failed to deliver?			
2	What went wrong?			
3	Is anything wrong with my working style?			
4	Do I lack in a particular skill?			
5	Are my			

	emotions affecting my work?			

Stage –II: Finding the problem

In this stage, we will work to trace the golden triad of the problem. After writing the questions of golden triad under 'Questions' column you should honestly write the situations which caused them under 'Answers' column. How you could have avoided that situation should be mentioned under column 'Resolution'.

Sl. No.	Question	Answer	Resolution
1	What has happened?		
2	How it happened?		
3.	Why it happened?		

After successfully finding the appropriate answers and resolution towards the questions of golden triad, we need to put in our genuine efforts to learn new concepts in life in order to lead a much better, improved and successful life.

Stage – III: Learning new concepts

Sl. No.	Name of the new habit which you should learn	Progress after one week	Progress after 15 days	Progress after one month
1	Avoid seeking sympathies			
2	Never take situation			

	personally			
3	Never be emotionally driven			
4	Never hesitate to accept your failures.			
5	Any other habit which you think is appropriate to learn			

After successfully completing these three stages you should come back and write your personal observations regarding changes which you have observed in yourself and how these changes have benefitted your life.

____

____

____

____

____

____

____

____

____

____

...................................*** ....

Chapter-8

(Stop brooding)

"Brooding is one of the most useless and destructive exercise known to the mankind"

Monday morning's are often more taxing than rest of the week. The most complicated and challenging tasks are always assigned or kept pending by the senior management for the Monday morning's as if the employees, often considered inefficient by the management, are about to undergo a massive transformation during the weekend and they all are going to show up on Monday morning with exceptional enthusiasm, doubled energy and enhanced skills.

If it was up to me to decide, then I would have surely scheduled all the meetings and complicated tasks for Friday thus sparing my Mondays. Because I always know that no matter how my day is turning up but the evening is surely going to be great. Friday evenings are the best stress busters as it is the doorway to the most awaited weekend.

However, the fact of the matter is that I am having a very big and important presentation in the office on coming Monday. The entire presentation is focused on our new innovative, unique and state of the art software on automation which I am supposed to pitch to one of our high value clients. Rumors are there that this pitch may play a significant role in success of my carrier.

Apart from this presentation I am also supposed to attend a birthday party of my office colleague, this afternoon. This party is more of an executive event rather than a birthday party therefore, it is not possible for me to skip it.

Although, I never like to work on Sundays but this presentation has left me with no other option. Therefore, after having my breakfast, I quickly moved into my room and started working on my presentation. It was a tedious one and after putting in a lot of efforts, I was finally able to finish it off by the late afternoon. I was happy at my accomplishment but soon I realized that I am already late for the party.

I dressed up hurriedly and walked towards the main gate (meanwhile I was continuously mumbling to myself, "I am late today; I am always late, whenever I need to go somewhere. God, I should not have slept during the day")

My monologue was interrupted by the professor's words of wisdom, "Son, do not brood, brooding is not a god habit. You are on time and I know you will make it, so be calm." (In the haste, I had absolutely failed to notice the professor who was sitting on the sofa in the living room)

(Assessing the situation he did not lectured me further but simply tried to reassure me. I must admit, he knows his words and when to use them and how to use them, he knows it all. I left for party and somehow managed to reach there on time).

The stress of upcoming presentation was so overwhelming that I was not able to enjoy the party to the fullest. I have done countless presentations before but still whenever I am supposed to deliver one, it always feels like as if I am doing it for the first time.

(Although this habit of doing work as if you are doing it for the first time is good as far as preparations are concerned as it helps in ruling out any possibility of ignorance or carelessness but at the same time it affects the overall quality of your life and trust me, it affects very badly. However, I cannot help it, at least not now.) Therefore, after having a little interaction with all of the important people present in there, I decided to leave early.

All of my friends insisted me to stay but I refused as I was not willing to show up next morning with red eyes and dull brain especially before an important presentation.

While driving back to home, I failed to notice the broken bottles which were scattered all over the road and as a result I ended up damaging my front tyre. Finally, I managed to reach home after 2am.

What a disastrous day it was, I thought to myself but it was far from being over. After parking my car in the garage, I noticed another flat tyre and this time it was the rear one. With spare tyre already in use, it was for sure that I won't be able to drive to the office, tomorrow morning.

So, with the approaching dawn, everything was set for a start of another miserable day. I dragged my self into my room and fell asleep in no time.

Next morning when I wake up, a simple glance at the clock was sufficient to sent chilling sensations down the spine. It was 8am and I had to reach office by 9:00am to discuss my presentation with my boss before the final presentation with clients which was scheduled at 10:00am.

I hurried my way to the restroom, freshened up and by 8:15 I was all dressed up. I looked at my watch and mumbled praising, "That was quick. I think I might make it on time."

I quickly walked out of my room towards the dining area to have some breakfast before leaving for the office. Then a sudden realization changed everything. Once I remembered the condition of my car, I panicked. I quickly took out my phone and tried booking a cab but no one was available. I tried calling my friend but he has already left for the office. I tried all other options but everything went down in vain.

I entered the drawing room panicked, frustrated and was so busy talking to my self that I totally failed to notice the professor, who was sitting on arm chair reading news paper and having his morning tea.

When, I was about to leave the room, the professor broke my monologue and said, "Good morning son, how was your party? You look a little messed up today, is everything all right?

A sudden deluge of questions startled me; I replied a little agitated, "Good morning professor."

Lost in thoughts I walked towards the breakfast table and mumbled, "God knows whether I am going to make it today or not. I must have not attended that party or at least I should have remembered to switch on the alarm. I am always messed up. I am always late for one thing or the other."

I quickly gobbled up my butter toast and took few quick sips of coffee before placing the cup back on the table.

Listening to all of my mumbling the professor interrupted once again, and said, "Son, don't you know that brooding is a bad habit, and you should avoid it"?

I replied a little irritated, "Sir, I don't brood."

I paused for a while, calmed down a little and then said politely, "but what is wrong with the brooding? How is it bad? Isn't it just another way to vent out?"

Professor said while pointing towards the clock, "I think, it's not the time to explain, will talk about it in evening. Till then try your best not to brood"

As I glanced at the clock, I yelled, "Oh god, I am late. I should have avoided this discussion at this moment. What am I going to do today?

I hurried my way fumbling towards door, as I walked out of the door; I failed to notice a newly placed wooden artifact and bumped my knee on it. Since I had no time to pamper my leg, so I kept moving, dragging my leg and constantly criticized myself all the time for my inability to wake up early in the morning.

I was supposed to take public transport for the office, some how I managed to board bus with aching leg. During this continuous act of self-nagging I forget to call Mac., who was waiting for me near his home as I was supposed to pick him up.

I quickly called him up and briefed him about the situation. He quickly hired a taxi and soon he was on his way to the office. Finally, I managed to reach the office.

It was around 9:45 am, it means I was late but not so late. Things still appeared manageable until I realized that I forgot to bring the pen drive in which I have stored the presentation, which I had made yesterday.

It was a day full of suffering, humiliations, explanations and apologies; in the evening with utmost feelings of despair, helplessness, frustration and fatigue, I started back to home, where the professor was waiting for me.

On my way back to home, I decided that today I would definitely share my problems with professor, after all, he is a good friend of mine and above all, he is far more intelligent and learned person than majority of the people around me.

Taking in account his vast experience and deep knowledge on various aspects of life, it would be foolish on my part, if I do not learn anything significant from him. Even if his advices may not prove beneficial to me, still there is no harm in listening to him.

Before going back to home, I decided to go to the park to relax my self. I took few fast strides towards the park and tried to implement the principle of positive body language that professor had taught me last Friday.

I was amazed to notice that as soon as I started moving fast, keeping the chin up and shoulders straight I started feeling a bit relaxed and eased. I praised professor for his wisdom and settled my self comfortably under the banyan tree.

While I was busy thinking, suddenly someone patted on my shoulder and a voice followed the pat, "how are you this evening, young man?"

(I looked up and was surprised to see professor)

I replied, "I am fine sir, thank you for asking"

Professor, "But I do not think so, you look so wasted. What happened?"

"I am fine, just feeling a little tired, may be" I replied

"Come on, even a deaf can hear your screams, it's painted all over your face. Say it boy what is it, that is bothering you?" professor asked in a concerned tone

(This time I decided to open up and thought that a lecture from the old man would not be bitterer than the scolding and disrespect which I got today for being a looser and for having an unprofessional and careless attitude towards the work.)

I said, "Sir, speaking honestly I myself don't know what is wrong with me, I work hard but... (I paused for a moment and looked anxiously at old man)

Professor said in a concerned tone, "Speak up son, do not stop. I am willing to listen to you, speak up, I am all ears."

(I continued but tried not to look at him while speaking) I said, "I work hard and try my best to meet every deadline but I always fail, no matter what I do and how honestly I might have done it but still I fails. It seems that failure is my destiny and I am being chosen by the god for all of this suffering. Let's discuss about today, I missed my alarm, hurt my leg, forget to call my friend and above all left the pen drive in home, that pen drive in which I have stored the presentation. And the outcome was obvious; I was not able to give the presentation on which

I was working from days and instead of getting appreciation for my work, I was scolded for my carelessness and unprofessional attitude."

I continued further and said, "I know, I am not careless but don't know how to prove it to others, now this thing is getting on to my nerves. I really can not understand what is wrong with me, sometimes I also feel now that may be I am not that good or may be their opinion about me is right"……………..(I paused after saying this and looked into eyes of professor as I was seeking an answer for my questions).

Professor replied calmly, "Listen young man I know what is wrong with you and I am willing to tell you that but I have one condition."

I asked inquisitively, "What is it?"

I regained my clam and continued jokingly, "do I need to buy a bottle of wine for you?"

Professor smiled back and replied, "No, all you have to do is to listen to me carefully and that too without getting emotionally involved or taking things personally.

 I am here to help you and not to scold you. When I will speak to you, you will listen to me as if you are listening to some other person's story who is seeking help from you and after listening to the story you will help in sorting the answers for his questions"

The condition looked a little weird but I accepted it and said, "It is ok with me, and seems like fun too. Please speak out what ever you want to".

Professor took a seat beside me and said while explaining to me, "Problem is not with you or with your dedication, nor is with your hard work or with your abilities, they are all good. Trust me, I have observed you for days, you are a brilliant, talented, well behaved and a patient person".

He continued and said, "Above all you are smart, honest, and a dedicated worker."

Listening to his sweet words, I interrupted him and said, "You are so kind and speaking all that can comfort me, thanks for that. But, I am ready to take hard blows, come on tell me what is wrong with me".

Professor appeared a little annoyed and said, "Look son, you are not abiding by your promise, and you have already started taking things personally. I think I need to stop."

His reaction surprised me, as I have never seen him this assertive, so I decided not to interrupt him. I said apologizing, "Please continue and I will take care of this".

Professor continued and said, "You have all the good qualities that one should posses that is why whenever someone scolds you, you do not accept it as true and put in your best efforts to prove him wrong. That undiminishing will of yours speaks a lot about your abilities".

But still you are losing again and again, no matter how hard you exert or better you perform but still one or other reasons often crept out of nowhere and ends up stealing the victory from you.

After facing this situation for few times, it's obvious for you to think that there must be something extremely wrong with you that is responsible for your failures and this negative thought is often reinforced by the supervisors whose main role appears to find a person who can be placed in the direct line of fire.

In spite of repeated sessions of introspection you are not able to find out the vice in you which is causing all of this trouble."

He was speaking my heart out. I wanted him to continue as I was eager to know the reason which was holding me back. I wanted to ask but then I remembered his diktat and stayed silent.

He continued with his monologue and said, "This vice is your habit of brooding, yes a very innocuous looking habit of yours."

I interrupted instantaneously and said surprisingly – What! Brooding? How, it can be? Please explain this to me I am not able to understand this."

Professor replied, "Yes I will explain it for you and would try to keep it short and simple".

He continued and said, "I am not talking about you or about anyone specific. Unfortunately all of us, which includes the people around you whom you know or work with and those unfamiliar faces which we see on roads, buses and other public places.

All of us have this habit. We all have been groomed by the society in such a way that instead of accepting and facing our problems we tend to shy away.

We have become so self centered and fragile that we tend to shy away from almost each and every responsibility. Forget about volunteering ourselves or helping anyone, we don't even want to get involved in any work other than the task assigned to us.

This innocuous looking habit subconsciously leads to the development of a weak mindset and hence encourages us to shy away from our problems.

A weak mindset will never allow us to own our mistakes, forget about rectifying them and finding solutions.

This simple habit has transformed us into such a weaklings, that only few among us have been left with the confidence and strength to stand up for our self and speak out loud that, "**yes I was wrong and have committed this mistake. I am sorry for that but I assure you that I will put in my earnest efforts to make up to your loss. You can count on me.**"

Whether you like it or not, a mistake is a mistake and it stays there until it is rectified. It is not possible to hide a mistake forever; sooner or later it will get pointed out.

Therefore, it's always better to own the one which you have committed instead of looking for the ways to hide it.

Such simple words of confession, commitment and resolute can bring peace at once to our mind but it seems that we all have taken an unending oath to not utter a single simple word in our life.

Instead, we keep on equivocating and unrelentingly trying to hide our mistakes and faults behind the misleading half truths and false clarifications with sole intent to justify the absolutely indefensible.

As a result, we often end up arguing with everyone including our self. Soon we are so deep in to this process of fault finding and denial that we are always ready with an explanation for what has happened and sometimes even for the events which are yet to happen.

Over a period of time we become so accustomed with our state of denial that we are always ready with an explanation beforehand, no matter what the situation is.

 Soon this habit manifests further deep down and now we are into the next step and that is the blame game.

In this step we start with blaming anyone other than ourselves for the mistake. Usually we start with our coworker or immediate junior and sometimes even our immediate senior, if he happens to not have a good rapport with the senior management.

However, a stage comes when no one else is left to blame and at that point we start blaming our self for whatever wrong is happening around us or has happened with us. This is the point where we achieve a new low in our life.

We are not willing to accept the responsibility of our actions and often end up criticizing our self for almost everything wrong happening around us.

Sometimes this unrelenting criticism lasts for the lifetime especially for some of our decisions or actions that went wrong and as per our own expert opinion we failed only and only due to that decision or action.

No matter what our present is and how many other factors might have played their role in influencing and shaping it; but still whenever we will start an avalanche of introspection, the responsibility of the failure will lay with us and on that one single decision of ours that went wrong?

This tendency of repeatedly revisiting and reliving the lowest moments of our life without applying any logic or mind to the circumstances which had lead to that event/occurrence or situation is brooding!

Brooding is one of the most useless and destructive exercise known to the mankind. It has an innate potential to keep us low, depressed, inactive, unproductive and unhealthy.

Brooding is the most common habit among all of us; it varies in its intensity but is almost universal in its presence. Invariably everyone (young or old, male or female) broods, it seems like brooding is indispensable for us and we cannot afford to live without it.

Often people brood but are either unaware of it or do not accept it. Whatever may be the situation, the fact is that we are nourishing a parasite with in us, which has a crippling effect on our efficiency, abilities, mental health, physical health and social health.

☞ **Let us discuss the effects of brooding:-**

⇨ Brooding keeps our mind always preoccupied with the futile thoughts, as a result of which we often experience fatigue without doing any work.

⇨   It becomes very difficult for us to think imaginatively and creatively.

⇨   Our concentration levels drops significantly and we find it very difficult to work with focus or to deliver any quality work in a time bound manner.

⇨   It affects our memory and attention span.

⇨ This innocuous looking activity has potential of making considerable transformations in our character.

➡ It makes us to forget about our potentials, abilities, skills, dreams, and commitments; only thing which we remember now is that negative thought or the event which we are brooding over."

Professor looked at me and said, "Earlier you had asked me a question, that what is wrong with you?"

He got up, I was quick to follow. He said while placing his hand on my shoulder, "Son there is nothing wrong with you, you are a wonderful young man with abilities and a good character, all you need is to learn to tame your thinking process and stop brooding. Have some courage to accept your mistakes and put in your 100% efforts to rectify them."

He said cheerfully, "So young man, from now onwards don't criticize yourself even if you wake up late or come home late after attending a party or work.

Just learn to spare your mind of this misery and let yourself see the positive part of life."

He said concluding, "Just learn your lessons and forget the past. Live in present and make optimum use of your mind to handle the challenges of today and the requirements of future.

Never ever waste your time, energy and mind in analyzing the events of past for forever; it won't yield anything useful to you."

After completing his lecture, he smiled at me and said, "Now you are free to ask anything that you want to know?"

I replied, "Sir, I don't think that there is anything left unanswered. I am feeling much better now; thank you very much for your advice."

I continued and said, "professor did you remember you were telling me about your life that night?"

Professor replied in affirmation

I continued and said, "That night, when I went to the bed, I realized that if we made few changes in your story then your story becomes my biography. I am suffering the same what you had suffered, I have a certain believe that you can help me to tide over this phase of my life"

"I will teach you what all life has taught me, with a profound hope that these principles and methods which once worked for me will also work for you" Professor replied.

After listening to those comforting words, I thanked him from the core of my heart. His advises were realistic, methods were workable and his philosophy was straightforward. Unable to find suitable words to thank him and express my gratitude, I simply smiled back at him.

Professor said, "I think it's time to move now. Aren't you having office tomorrow?"

"Certainly professor, in fact I haven't eaten food since morning. I am starving." I replied as we started walking towards the home.

We had our dinner and then we were having a light conversation over a cup of hot coffee. I was feeling much relaxed, energetic and most importantly optimistic towards the life.

I was quite happy with this makeover of mine and was truly grateful for the professor for sharing his immense knowledge and valuable experiences with me.

While having the conversation, professor got up from his recliner walked up to his bag and took out something from the inside pocket of the bag. It appeared like a booklet.

He said while giving it to me, "I think you should read this, you might find it interesting or may be even useful"

"Sure, I will love to read it" I replied as I took it from him. It was a note pad. I quickly flipped through its pages and placed it on the armrest of my sofa chair.

After having a little discussion on random topics we called it the day and moved towards our bedrooms.

···❋❋❋···

What to do?

 Control your thinking process.

➡ Apply all the principles and methods which we have learnt earlier, so that we are able to restrict and control the movement of thoughts in and out of our mind.

➡ With regulated movement of thoughts we will be able to think better and work on the useful ideas to get desired results.

➡ This will save a lot of our time, energy and our resources thus making us more productive, popular and progressive.

➡ Whenever you are faced with a challenging situation, you should avoid jumping to the conclusion, as by doing so you will be able to extract a little extra time necessary to understand what has happened.

➡ Write down the problem or the cause of distress in a distress management section of the notebook/ ThinkPad.

➡ Now perform the detailed dissection of the situation or problem to arrive at the golden triad of the problem.

➡ Once you have arrived at the golden triad then channelize your thought process to find suitable answers to mitigate the situation and to ensure that it must not recur in future.

➡ While doing detailed analysis of the situation, if you happen to find out any shortcoming in your personality or in your skills then make sure to work on it.

⇨ Once you will start handling the problems logically and practically, your mind will be full of creativity and positivity with no time left for negative activities like brooding.

☞ **Make the following detailed chart:-**

Sl. No	Question	Your answer
1.	What am I thinking about?	
2.	Is it worth thinking?	
3.	Why I am thinking about this?	
4.	What caused this problem or situation to arise?	
5.	Are there any influencing factors which need to be addressed?	
6.	What all difficulties I may have to face while addressing this situation/ problem?	
7.	Am I lacking somewhere?	
8.	Did I miss any significant details?	

My conclusion____

____

____

....✹✹✹..

Chapter-9

(Stop acquiring sympathies)

"Sympathies are not meant for achiever"

I Walked inside my room, placed the notepad on the bed and went inside bathroom to freshen up. The weather was getting colder, so I rekindled the fire in the fireplace and sat on the sofa placed beside it.

I picked up the note pad and quickly flipped through its pages. It had few topics written on it. I decided to start with the first topic and it goes like this

☞ *Stop acquiring sympathies*

It is beyond doubt that the words of sympathy appears as elixir to the aching ego.

⇨ However, whenever I think about sympathy following questions often come across my mind:

> ➤ **Why we need sympathy?**

> ➤ **What good or bad it does to us?** And most importantly

> ➤ **Do we really need sympathies, at all?**

Leaving all the theories aside, what I feel is that the sympathy is nothing more than a reassurance given to you, by the people around you to reconfirm that, yes! Something bad has happened to you and you are at a great loss.

Of course, none of them really mean it, but still they say this to simply please your ears.

☞ Why do we seek sympathy?

We seek sympathy because we want to hear the words which speak of our innocence and describe injustice that has happened to us. These words appear soothing to us as everyone is speaking exactly what we want to hear about.

When we are successful and on the top, at that moment if asked, we often say that everything which we have achieved in life is mainly due to our hard work, dedication, commitment and ability to snatch victory by putting up a tough fight against hardships and adversaries. We give a very little accreditation to the destiny or circumstances. There is nothing wrong in doing that, as every effort needs to be appreciated.

However, when we are facing downfall in life, things change and so do our perception and thoughts. Now instead of accepting the responsibility for our failure and trying to analyze it in detail, (what went wrong and how it went wrong), we sort refuge in denial.

We prefer to surround ourselves with sympathizers, as our ears are aching to hear these assuring words **"it is not your fault, it was destiny"** or even a better excuse that **"someone else is somehow responsible for this and in fact, you are just another innocent lamb being crucified"**.

It appears as if we are training our mind to believe that the failure has been imposed by destiny on us whereas victory is the one that we snatch from the clutches of destiny.

Isn't this a little irrational way to generalize failures? How are we not at all accountable for our losses? In reality we are. However we seldom prefer to acknowledge it, forget about accepting this fact.

No matter what the reality is or what wrong we have done, we all firmly believe in the fact that the innocence is our innate right.

☞ What harm sympathies do to us?

Now, when we are not at all willing to accept the reality of the situation then there is no much room left for the analysis or self-improvement.

Now, when we have already developed an immunity towards the accountability and have neither the scope nor the desire left for self-improvement then what else do we need to hear other than the soothing words of sympathies to please our ears and to reassure us of our innocence and helplessness.

Unfortunately, we never ever bother to see what all damages we are doing to our self by developing an inclination towards sympathies. By paying heed to the sympathies we not only reduce the chances of our success but also adversely affect our self-esteem and self-confidence, which I think, is quite a heavy price to pay, merely to defend or deny a mistake or failure.

Things do not end here, while traversing this soothing escape route we find ourselves trapped in the vicious cycle of failure followed by sympathies.

Due to our repeated denial and dodging of the accountability, soon our mind fails to ascertain what to do when ever we are faced with a challenging situation, leaving us clueless and miserable.

 Now, we have only one virtue left with us, and that is, **'the blame game'**. Oh! I forgot to mention another one and that is **'the cries for help'**, which only grew louder with time and soon people start developing deaf ears towards such cries; this indifference further induces stress and frustration within us.

When we tend to increase an acceptance towards sympathy, we start depleting our self-esteem and confidence due to which our faith in self become insubstantial. Our thinking becomes fragile and the will to improve is now almost an obsolete concept for us.

We cannot think of anything remedial or innovative. Our patience starts wearing away and heart starts sinking in unexplainable fears. We are dying to speak to a sympathizer who can hear us out and can shed few tears on our miseries to make us feel that our loss is real.

By accepting the sympathy from others, we are carving a coward out of us, and are therefore unable to fend off our vice.

Gradually we start developing a dependence on others for acquiring mental peace and comfort, we start talking about our miseries loudly and so frequently that soon we actually become miserable.

In our absence, understandably many of our sympathizers brand us as a childish, idiot, coward, looser and an unreliable person of very demanding nature, who is always up with one or another reason for crying.

Why we are unable to understand this very simple fact that the sympathies are not the solutions and neither are they any quick fixes, which will spell something magical and will increase our ability to fight and survive.

Sympathy will not and cannot compensate for your loss however; it may further make you feel worse by reiterating the fact that you have lost something very important.

☞ What should be done?

Stop acquiring sympathies as they only weaken you from inside and unknowingly forces you to lose your credibility.

Instead of seeking for sympathies, make yourself -strong, re-establish your faith in self and say no to the sympathizers. Remember one thing that, it's you and only you who can help yourself.

Whenever things go wrong or we are in trouble, most of us try to console our self and there is nothing wrong in it, till it is kept within the confines of our heart.

If you want sympathy then sympathize yourself by achieving something remarkable, if you have lost someone do something to make his/ her memories memorable.

Whenever you lose, instead of seeking out for sympathy seek an explanation from yourself why this happened and what you could have done to avoid it.

Do not let the people surround you and do R&D on you, as this will not only waste your precious time but it also drains a lot of energy out of you.

You have lost what you have lost! It would not come back. The mistake committed by you is done and once it's done it cannot be undone. The best we can do is to try not to repeat the same mistake in future.

☞ Always remember this golden rule

'Sympathies are not meant for achievers' because achievers don't have time to mourn rather they learn from their losses and mistakes, more they lose more determined they become.

Moreover 'sympathies can never ever help a loser', as he cannot think beyond the loss.

It is far better to try to learn from your loss rather then wasting your time in seeking sympathies and rendering your self vulnerable to manipulations and suggestions.

What an outstanding and informative piece of writing it was. I have never thought on these lines before. I closed the note pad and placed it on the table. I switched off the lights and closed my eyes.

What I had just read was echoing inside my mind.

I tried to introspect a little and I realized that professor is right about sympathies. Whenever someone offers sympathy to me, I often became a little more tensed and depressed especially when that person leaves and I am on my own, as the same thought of failure keep on coming in mind again and again. Making me exhausted and fatigued.

He is also right in saying that these so called sympathizers, often makes fun of the person (behind his back) who they are sympathizing with. He is not more than a pathetic individual with no intelligence, self respect or dignity for them. These people even don't hesitate to manipulate and sometimes even emotionally blackmail such person.

I was feeling much enlightened, relaxed and content. I was sure that I was going to get a good night sleep tonight and it proved right.

Next morning when I went to the office, everyone was looking at me with sympathetic eyes and were willing to console me for my failure at the presentation.

I felt like a miserable mouse surrounded by lot of cats ready to pounce on me. However, they all were shocked and surprised to see my changed attitude.

Whenever somebody approached to console me; I simply smiled and would start talking on some altogether different topic with a lot of enthusiasm and spirit.

In case a person is still able to strike the right note I would just say, "It happens sometimes, failure is just another part of life, and I am ok with it."

Soon I was surprised to overhear them at water cooler where they were praising me for my courage, positive approach and strong mindset.

I smiled and moved back to my seat and mumbled, "Just a little change in behavior is sufficient to yield exponential results"

The professor's article was not only enlightening but realistic and reliable. It worked for me and I am sure it would work for anyone who would like to put his mind into the work instead of emotions.

I was happy and thrilled to see how the day worked out for me. I was eager to share this with professor, so as I reached home, first thing that I did was to search for him in the study but he was not there.

I asked Jerry as I placed my bag on a chair next to the study, "Where is professor? Hasn't he returned yet?"

"He left for some meeting, almost an hour ago" jerry replied as he glanced at his watch.

I asked jerry to prepare a cup of hot coffee for me and I quickly walked to my room to get that notepad. I was eager to read what else he had written inside it.

✳ ✳ ✳

What to do?

☞ **Step-1**; **Learn to be a little secretive**; a little secrecy is always helpful.

⇨ Make the following chart to know whether you can maintain secrecy or not

Sl. No.	Question	Your answer
1.	Do I have access to any privileged or important information today?	
2.	Did I share it with anyone?	
3.	Were he/ she tried to elicit the information from me?	
4.	Whether I divulged the information myself?	
5.	Was I trying to boast?	
6	Did I pass on the information unknowingly?	
7.	Am I too talkative?	

Once you have answered all of the above questions, it will be quite easy for you to know whether you can maintain secrecy or not.

2. In case, the answer to most of the questions above, is yes than at least now you are already aware of your limitations and can practice restrain in future while entering in conversations.

It would be much better if you could track your progress for almost a month in above format. With conscious efforts and intent you will see a gradual improvement in yourself.

☞ **Step-2**: **Avoid unnecessary conversations especially at work.** Because most of the times the most important information is often divulged during the least important conversations.

☞ **Step-3**: **Don't talk about your failures;**

Instead of talking about your failures treat them as your stepping stones. We all have heard this phrase "failures are the stepping stones of success" however most of us don't know how to achieve this is reality, and how to learn from our mistakes and failures.

The very basic requirement of any learning is to have the proper understanding of the subject. So in order to learn from our failures, we first need to understand them thoroughly so that we are able to extract useful information and learning from our failures, which can be used subsequently.

We should make this failure assessment sheet in our dairy

Sl. No.	Question	Your answer
1.	Did I fail?	
2.	Why did I fail?	
3.	Was the task beyond my capabilities?	
	If yes,	
	a) then what are the areas in which I am lacking	
	b) what all I can do to overcome this	
	If no, a) then what lead to this failure	

4.	Was this failure preventable?	
5	How could I have prevented this failure?	
6.	Has this happened before?	

➤ After answering all of the above questions carefully and honestly, try to summarize the entire incidence like what happened, how it happened and how it has affected you?

____

____

____

____

➤ Now when you have the clear picture of the failure with you, now write down how you intend to overcome your limitations and emerge out as a winner in next encounter:

____

____

➤ Note down the take away points which you got from this incidence and the learning which you want to retain and use in future situations. This is the most important aspect of this exercise. Write the take away points in the following space:

____

____

____

____

Now you will be able to use your failure as a stepping stone.

....✳✳✳...

Chapter – 10

(Master your Emotions)

"Emotions are the least understood yet over utilized resources know to
the mankind"

I Took the notepad with me and climbed up the stairs to the terrace. It was almost an hour to sunset, so I decided to read while basking in sun. I made myself comfortable on a recliner meanwhile jerry served a cup of coffee to me.

I placed the cup on the adjoining table and opened the notepad to read the next topic, which goes like this:

Never be emotionally driven

Emotions, although it is a very small word in itself, yet it represents an extensive spectrum of feelings ranging from happiness to sorrow, from pride to jealousy, from contentment to anxiety, from courage to fear, from greed to hope and from envy to desire.

Our identity itself is a subtle expression of our emotions. Our emotions and the manner in which we express them often define our personality and to some extent our ideologies too. In fact, we all are surrounded by an aura of emotions throughout our lives.

Emotions when utilized in favor can bring success but when left unguided and on their own, they can lead to a devastating defeat.

God bestowed emotion upon us so that we can feel the essence of humanity and make our life richer, happier, and livable.

Emotions are the least understood yet over utilized resources know to the mankind. Often we use our emotions indiscriminately without realizing the power contained in them and the extent to which they can influence our thoughts, actions and capabilities.

☞ Let us see how emotions control our actions and influence our responses:

⇨ **Stage-I: Influences our judgment:**

➤ Emotions influence our state of mind which in turn determines our mood. Our mood affects how we are going to judge any situation, when presented to us.

➤ Our judgment is going to play a decisive role in determining our response to any situation.

⇨ **Stage–II: Guides our response to any situation:**

➤ Whenever we are emotionally excited we feel spurts of energy from within which are often accompanied by a resoundingly high confidence level.

➤ This surging confidence level is invariably accompanied by an extraordinary willingness to accept almost any task, blame it on the adrenaline rush or the immense emotional potential which influences our judgment and somehow manages us to overstep our true potential.

➤ Therefore, we often end up committing to something reasonably over demanding and sometimes even unachievable.

➤ Whereas on the downside of it, when we are depressed, even an ordinary looking task appears to be insurmountable. We feel that we are the only useless person alive on this planet, who cannot accomplish anything of reasonable importance in his life.

➤ Factually, we all know that this is too low than our actual potential, but still our emotions manipulate us in believing this stupid idea and gradually we start feeling depressed, lonely and unrequired.

⇨ **Stage-III: Makes us unpredictable and hence unreliable:**

➤ Emotions often trigger a chain reaction which can go in either direction.

➤ When we are unable to tame and control our emotions, we cannot control the outcome. Hence, understandably we will become less predictable for the people around us because our response to a single stimulus will be different on different occasions, depending on our mood.

➤ When our responses are not based on certain logical and concrete principles and ideologies, there is a significant chance of making a bad or even wrong decision.

➤ Too many wrong decisions reduce our reliability and understandably, people start doubting out skills and capabilities.

⇨ **Stage- IV: Blocking logical thought process:**

➤ Emotions acts like barricades blocking the logical thought process that occurs inside our brain.

➤ That's not all; our emotions even exert their best to try to ward off any influence of brain in the decision making process and by doing so they give rise to unnecessary conflicts in between logic and feelings.

➤ Such conflicts often adds to the confusion and ultimately ends up diluting the level of our conviction, thereby making it very difficult to execute the proposed plan with a whole- hearted attempt.

➤ Such compromised and half hearted attempts often make it reasonably difficult for us to achieve our goals. Hence, we are faced with failures.

➤ Sometimes, even the projects or the assignments in which we are confident of achieving success, fails due to these untimely and unrequired conflicts in thoughts and confusions in execution.

➤ Even in a discussion, the person who is better able to manage his emotions often turns out to be the winner than the one who acceded to his feelings.

It is clear by now that no matter whether we are happy or sad, our emotions induces an illusionary and euphoric state of mind, thus impairing and interfering with our normal decision making processes.

Whatever we may think, decide or commit under the impression and influence of our emotions, it has its own repercussions; which we have to face subsequently.

Doubtlessly, our emotions are our most priced possessions, but we need to learn to keep them at bay while conceptualizing, planning, executing, analyzing and evaluating our work.

☛ **We need to learn and understand that emotions are short lived, but the task which we accept or plan to perform under the influence of the emotions has long term commitments and consequences.**

☛ **Always remember, it is not possible for a short term input like emotion to guide us through a long term endeavor to achieve success in life?**

Commitments, which are done in rage or under the influence of emotion are often bound to fail, further leaving us devastated, agitated, depressed and sometimes even broke.

☛ **How should we make our decisions?**

⇨ We need to understand that our decisions must not be guided and our actions must not be controlled by our emotions, instead of allowing emotions to influence each and every important decision of our lives, we should learn to control our emotions.

⇨ We must ensure to plan our work based on a logical thinking and a rational approach.

⇨ With logical approach we are better able to consider every minute detail of the work to be accomplished and scrutinize every possible source of error before making any final commitment.

⇨ Logical approach towards work provides us with a strong foundation, which is immune to the emotional turmoil that may strike in between the ongoing action.

⇨ We need a relaxed and peaceful mind to make plans and successfully execute them.

A person who accedes to his emotions cannot acquire a stable, unbiased and peaceful state of mind.

God bestowed us with this wide range of immense emotional fortune so that we can live a more meaningful life by understanding the needs and miseries of people surrounding us and reaching out to them with help, in the hour of need, in any possible way.

Emotions enable us to feel the warmth of love, compassionateness of friendship, joy of giving and ultimately living a much fuller and happier life.

At the same time, God also gifted humans with a brain blessed with special abilities like logic and analytical skills so that we can acquire experience and are better able to utilize this experience when need arises.

Thereby making us more efficient and capable of making logical, practical and executable decisions, which are when executed meticulously, will lead us to the success and will help us in achieving gratifying results.

However, what we do in real life is just opposite to what the God might have expected from us. We mostly end up mixing emotions with work, thereby creating a never ending battery of troubles, failures, losses and heartburns.

This mix-up happens purely due of our inability to separate the working of brain and heart i.e. the logic and the emotions.

☞ What happens when we mix-up emotions and work

⇨ We often end up mixing emotions with work, and logic in relationships. As a result, as the day progresses our stress level start shooting up and gradually we end up as a complaining individual with aching careers and soaring relationships.

➡ Work related stress and disturbed family relations are becoming almost universal in occurrence and almost every person is down with one or both of these problems.

All of this is happening because we have really messed up the things.

☞ Let us first begin with the effects of this mix-up at work place:

➡ For instance, at work place where we are facing wrath of the deadlines, managing overtaxing work load and are answerable to a very strict boss; usually in such scenario we are expected to get fatigued, exhausted and tired as our brain and body is expected to work for long hours. However, in office we often feel more stressed out and irritated rather than fatigued.

➡ Point worth considering here is that, in general it's the brain which gets tired, exhausted and fatigued after working for long hours, whereas it is our mind which deals with the entire emotional endeavor like stress, frustration and irritation etc.

➡ Logically there is no reason to feel stress at work, as this can happen only if you are letting your emotions to interfere in your work, your emotions of fear, rivalry, jealousy and greed makes you miserable.

➡ When this happens, gradually you start focusing more into the office politics rather than giving your undivided attention to your work.

➡ No doubt, if you yourself managed to achieve success by manipulations and by indulging in office politics, then you are bound to get heartburns on the success of others.

☛ **Now let's talk about the effects of this mix-up in our personal life:**

➡ Earlier, you were stressed in the office and now you feel fatigued, exhausted and tired on reaching home.

➡ Since you have already utilized your emotional stocks in managing the work place politics, gossips and criticizing others therefore nothing much is left to share with your spouse or friends when you reach home already preoccupied with your office politics.

➡ However, after reaching home you are full of logical explanations and arguments (which originate in brain and not in heart or mind) and you often end up arguing with your spouse or loved ones, over very minor issues.

Now you start blaming your friend or spouse by accusing them, by saying that "they do not understand or even try to understand you".

➡ However, in reality it's you, who never bother to think what if, they are using their heart and emotions to think and interact especially with you and are expecting the same in return from you.

What is wrong in using heart instead of using brain in personal life; as you are not here to negotiate a profitable deal with your spouse, are you?

We need to know and understand where to love and where to compete.

⇒ We are so messed up with our emotions that we often lose track of them. Gradually a time comes when we are no longer in control of our emotions but have become a slave to them. We appear to have simply lost the ability to strike a balance between logic and emotions.

⇒ As a result, our emotions force us to commit mistakes and our brain compels us to repent for the mistakes committed by us. This leads to an unending inner conflict, thereby making life miserable for us as well as for the people around us.

Unfortunately, we have reduced ourselves to mere puppets playing in the hands of what we were destined to own and control.

☞ **Now question arises how to use our emotions to the best of our interests and keep them out of play when they are not required?**

The answer to this question is very simple and it lies within us. We just need to follow few steps and over period of time by repeated practice we will be able to master our emotions.

⇒ **Step –I: learn to stay in the character:**

➤ When god has attributed various roles to us like that of a, businessmen/ businesswomen, an employer on an employee, a father/ mother, brother/sister and husband/ wife and all of these coexist amicably; therefore, we also need to program ourselves to stay in the character which we are performing at a given point of time.

➤ At work place behave, act, listen, speak, analyze, understand and respond like a true and committed businessperson.

➤ At home, behave like a caring and responsible parent, committed and loving spouse, and a willing and helping friend.

➤ You just have to learn to give appropriate importance to every relationship that exists in your life.

➤ After putting in sincere efforts for few days you will be able to see a spontaneous transition in our behavior and in our responses.

➤ You need to understand this clearly that purpose of this exercise is not merely role playing or trying to pretend someone else, rather this exercise is just a humble attempt to restore the lost work and life balance.

➤ Unfortunately, deeply entangled in building our careers and amassing comforts for self and family we have almost forgotten every other aspect of our life and relationships.

Therefore this role play is necessary to reclaim the lost relationships and responsibilities which unknowingly got outsourced since long, in this rat race.

➤ After putting in the genuine efforts for initial few days every relationship of yours will start falling in line and that too without putting in any extra efforts.

Gradually you will be able to enjoy the true warmth and comfort of any and almost every relationship which you have.

This will help significantly in countering the work related stress as you will be able to spend few hours of absolutely stress free quality time with your near and dear ones.

⇨ **Step-II: Give equal importance to work as well as family**

➤ As no part of body can be dearer than the other, and all of them are required in a healthy state for the proper functioning of our body, similar is the case with the relationships; all are important in their own way and we need them all in a healthy state to live a meaningful life.

➤ Success sounds much sweeter when we have a family and friends around us to celebrate it, and situations appear less stressful when we have someone to confide in.

⇨ **Step-III: learn to strike a balance between logic and emotions**

➤ To succeed comprehensively in our personal and professional life, we needs to learn to strike a balance between logic and emotions, and are expected to play every character attributed to us with perfection.

⇨ **Step-IV: Never personalize any situation**

➤ Irrespective of the situation or the circumstances which lead you to the uncomfortable or stressful situation at work or at home, always remember that it is the event or the act which is under scrutiny and not you.

➤ Therefore, never ever take any situation personally. Most of the times, the responses given by people around us are subjective and they keep on changing based on our performance and their expectations from us.

➤ Therefore, instead of personalizing the situation and adding stress in your life, simply try to focus on the reason behind this shortfall, completely ignoring the response of the individuals.

Trust me, till today I was never able to understand why life is becoming miserable day after day for me. However, today after reading and understanding this article, I was able to get answers to many unanswered questions of my life, the questions, which have haunted me for long.

Now, it was clear to me that it is my unbalanced and rouge emotions, which keeps letting me down time and again. Further, my tendency of personalizing each and every situation only worsened the things for me.

The professor was quite true in saying that, "**Emotions are the least understood and over utilized resources, used by us, we use our emotions indiscriminately and that too without realizing the power imbibed in them and the extent to which they can influence our thoughts, action and capabilities**".

I closed the notepad and looked towards the horizon, the view was beautiful.

The professor was right in many aspects. Majority of our sufferings have an emotional reason attributed to them and most of the times problems start arising when we start taking the remarks and comments personally.

This habit of personalization often lands us, in unnecessary arguments and acts as a seeding ground for enmity, hatred and revenge.

....✱✱✱..

What to do?

Whenever you are faced with any stressful situation or any event which is capable of triggering a battery of emotions; instead of reacting instantaneously to that situation, try to do following:

☞ Relax.

☞ Try not to personalize the situation/ event.

☞ Don't discuss the issue with anyone yet, as you yourself are not fully aware of the situation.

☞ If possible, jot down all the expressions and emotions which are coming to your mind ____

____

____

____

____

☞ Now try to analyze each and every point which you have written down.

☞ Try to find out the golden triad of the problem.

     ➢ What has happened? ________________________

     ➢ How it happened? ________________________

     ➢ Why it happened? ________________________

☞ Summarize your problem and write the necessary details in the space clearly stating what the problem is _______________________________

____

____

____

☞ Now make a detailed note on what all possible damages it can cause to you

> At professional level _______________________________

____

> At personal level _______________________________

____

> How you are going to fix it

____

____

____

☞ Now when you are fully aware of what has happened, why it happened, and how it happened, then it becomes quite easier for you to rectify your mistake and do the needful corrections without subjecting yourself to any humiliation, degradation or emotional tantrum or trauma.

....✹✹✹..

Chapter-11

(Never take the situations personally)

"Most of our problems are having a single root cause and that
is our inability to keep our ego out of the play".

I Glanced at the watch, it was half past 4 and the professor was yet to return from his meeting. As I was having a little time with me so I decided to go ahead with the next topic, because I was finding his research quite interesting to read. The next topic goes like this:

"Never take the situations personally"

The Aching egos:

⇨ We all tend to take personally, any unpleasant communication conveyed to us or incident which might have happened at the work place, purely due to professional reasons.

⇨ Things don't end here; we often end up attaching emotional rants against the person involved in that episode. Although, we may not express our reservations against that person instantly, but they are there and whenever we are going to interact with that person in near future, this emotional legacy is invariably going to influence and affect our future interactions with that person.

⇨ Simply owing to this habit of taking things personally, we often spend many sleepless nights tossing in our bed, just planning and planning with sole motive to settle the score with that person.

⇨ In-fact, we are doing all of this to pacify our aching ego. This preoccupied state of mind leads to compromised levels of mental alertness at work and disharmony in our personal life.

☞ **Let us try to understand how this habit of taking things personally actually manifest itself and ends up affecting the quality of our professional and personal life.**

⇨ **The first response:**

➤ Every action potent enough to bring about significant effect in one's life often begins with an initial response, the first response.

➤ No matter what we are dealing with or what the situation might be, but mostly our initial response to any demanding or challenging situation is, fear.

➤ It doesn't matter whether we are being accused of something or the outcome of our efforts has failed to generate the desired results; whenever we heard about a rumor or news having our name in it, we become fearful.

➤ We don't know yet what has happened, why it has happened or how we are involved in it but still almost in a blink of an eye we become deeply infested with the fear of unknown.

➤ It's quite natural to have fear as our initial response because on the very outset of the problem, we are often unaware of its actual cause, the intensity and the extent of damage which this problem or situation might inflict on us.

➤ In absence of any confirmed information about the incidence, an element of uncertainty complemented by lots of, ifs and buts often clouds our judgment.

➤ This uncertainty leads to fear.

Now I will talk about the second stage, i.e. what happens after the fear steps in;

☛ **Consequences of fear:**

⇨ Fear leads to panic.

⇨ Panic is a single word commonly used to represent a group of expressions which are presented by our body and mind when being subjected to any unexplained fear, forcing us to believe that worse is going to happen with us. These are the moments when our mind completely forgets about logic and rational approach.

➡ Capitalizing on this panicked state of mind, our fears manipulates our thoughts in projecting the situation or the possible outcomes of any event, in a manner which is absolutely out-of–the proportion, especially when compared to the magnitude of the actual situation or incident.

➡ This heightened state of anxiety totally obscures the ability of our brain to think rationally, and therefore further limiting our chances of arriving at some suitable solution to address the situation appropriately.

➡ Often this is the most vulnerable state of mind in which we are bound to commit most serious mistakes.

➡ At this moment of vulnerability even on slightest of provocation, we lose our temper and feel like breaking his or her jaw into tiny fragments and if provoked further we might actually not refrain from indulging in a full fledge argument or even a fight, in worse cases.

➡ Often for most of us, things don't end here; in fact, it's just the beginning. Now we don't refrain from indulging in any form of revenge full activities like back- stabbing, lobbying and even disdainful gossips, all these disgraceful actives are done with the sole purpose of soothing our aching egos.

➡ While indulging in these destructive activities we achieve a new low in our life by dragging down our self esteem to such trivial levels that even a miniscule appearing altercation becomes sufficiently big enough for us to be considered as a prestige issue, subsequently we never misses a chance to fight back even over minor issues.

➡ It is natural to panic and frankly speaking there is nothing wrong in it. However, to stay in the state of panic for long is what causes the problems to start creeping up and soon these problems become so deep rooted, strong and intermingled that we find it very difficult to get rid of them.

➡ Unfortunately, this entire ruckus created by us does not go unnoticed and causes a substantial damage to our image at our work place as well as in our personal life.

➡ Soon people start recognizing us as a quarrelsome person, who is very difficult to work with. Now, no one wants us in his/ her team, no matter how much talented we are but now everyone around seems to start keeping a little distance from us.

➡ Still we are not able to make out what is going wrong and why is it happening with us. Ignoring our own mistakes which lead to this fallout in first place, we start considering this outcome as a result of office politics. Consequently we don't refrain from entering in a cold war type situation with that colleague, this act of ours starts consolidating the negative perception of people against us.

➡ Have you ever tried to sort out answer to the following questions?

> Why we are not as popular as some other person in the office?

➤ Why do people avoid to team up with us in spite of our abilities?

➤ Why we are not in a friendly terms with colleagues and neighbors?

All of our problems are having a single root cause and that is our inability to keep our ego out of the play.

We often end up by taking every single comment as a personal insult and start seeking revenge for it.

➡ We need to learn to generalize the things, there is no point in always taking the things personally and then reacting to them impulsively; as this scares the people around you and forces them to behave in a cautious manner, after all nobody likes to indulge in an argument.

➡ This cautious approach adopted by people infuriates us, further worsening the scenario.

➡ On the other hand, only if we can keep our highly esteemed and glorified personal image out of play, and learn to hear and interpret the words exactly in the manner and in the reference in which people had spoken them, without caring to add any additional meanings to them, we will make our life a lot easier and happier.

A person who is able to extract fun and laughter out of the conversation, instead of insult and humiliation, is all time favorite and is often admired by everyone for his humorous and understanding nature.

Interestingly, no one likes to challenge his efficiency.

In fact, people are happily willing to accommodate a little while working with such a vibrant person.

Now you can very well understand how little an effort is required to transform oneself from being an annoying person to most acceptable person, and how big a difference this transformation can create in one's life.

After all, it's our behavior and the manner in which we act, and reacts to our day to day interactions, is what creates all the difference.

⇨ Whatever might be the situation, there is no point in arguing as arguments only tarnishes your image.

⇨ If somebody has caused damage to you then instead of arguing and threatening him, try to balance his act as soon as possible. When there are numerous other ways to get even, why to waste energy and time in arguing.

⇨ Instead of wasting your energy and time in threatening and making your adversary aware that you may take revenge, just catch him unaware.

Remember that old saying, "barking dogs seldom bites" whereas a lion always keeps it stealth.

➡ Try hard not to involve in any altercation or fight, but if involved then do not let other person win, no matter what it takes but do not accede to his or her vicious intentions.

➡ Just keep using your brain instead of emotions and you will soon outwit your opponent.

➡ Lesser you show personal involvement; remote are the chances of you getting involved in any altercation or argument.

<table><tr><td>

Learn to work seriously and not personally.

As serious efforts will improve your efficiency at work, whereas personal involvement will give rise to unnecessary and unexpected conflicts with the people involved.

</td></tr></table>

It was a meaningful and worth learning aspect, which most of us overlook at our work places and often end up having arguments and conflicts.

By the time, I finished reading this article many of the problems which I face in my office seems to be addressed.

Now, I fully understand how and why I lose my temper in the office meetings when my team is criticized. And most importantly, why people in senior management prefer to consult the other executives rather than coming to me, especially when I am more efficient and resourceful than others.

Earlier, I was thinking of switching my job, as I was finding people manipulative and partial. But, now after reading and understanding this concept, I have changed my mind.

Now, I have decided to stick around and implement whatever I have learnt today and then will see how things work out for me.

***

What to do?

☞ Whenever you enter in any meeting or participate in a group discussion or interact with your colleagues, try not to get involved emotionally.

⇨ In order to achieve this, try to remember following rules and act accordingly:

> ➤ You are not the only intelligent person present in the room.

> ➤ It's a professional place so no one is going to bother about your feelings, sentiments and emotions.

> ➤ In any professional meeting, people are going to grill you for every little miniscule mistake of yours, so go fully prepared with logic and facts.

> ➤ Face every professional interaction with the same poise, patience, acumen, wit and confidence with which you had faced your job interview.

> ➤ Behave like a true professional and exhibit all of your professional qualities for which you were hired at the first place.

> ➤ People can have disagreement with you and they are allowed to convey their disagreement in the way they think it's appropriate.

> ➤ If you find their way of expression inappropriate then instead of complaining like a loser, wait for your turn. When they express something which is disagreeable then you can sound your disapproval in the way you found it appropriate.

➤ If you are a team leader then you are supposed to speak on behalf of your team. As you are not supposed to take the entire credit of your teams efforts similarly you are also not supposed to act like a guiding angel and face the bullets to shield others, especially the undeserving ones.

➤ Let those undeserving person face the music. Remember loyalty, commitment and dedication is supposed to be protected, reared and nourished not the weeds who are out there only to exploit and embarrass.

➤ Remember to keep all of your emotions out of the way.

➤ You should firmly believe that whatever is being said or discussed is purely professional which needs a purely logical response, if any.

➤ Even if someone tries to deliberately unsettle you by saying something with an intention to hurt you sentiments, you must not come out of your role of a perfect and competent executive.

➤ Everyone has the same goal of achieving that top position, therefore, always remember that a colleague is a competition and even the point that he is your friend, cannot and will not change this fact.

··❋❋❋···

Chapter - 12

(Habit of Denial)

"There is no way to hide a mistake, if you will not accept it by today, people around you will do their best to make you accept it by tomorrow."

As I further flipped through the pages I found this article, the title itself was conveying an assuring vibe to the reader. So, I quickly started reading this one and it went like this:

"Never hesitate to accept your failure"

It is well said that, "Failures are the stepping stones of Success".

You will find several such inspiring quotes scribbled almost everywhere; from magazines to newspapers, almost everyone is publishing and selling these quotes. The best part of these quotes is that they never get old.

There must be something truly engaging and inspiring in these quotes which forces us to read them over and over again, and that too when we have already read them before, isn't?

We will have to accept the fact, that reading these quotes do mesmerizes us to some extent and often induces a surge of energy within; but as soon as the page is turned to sports and entertainment segment the hypnosis starts fading away and the spurts induced within starts subsiding to the point of becoming nonexistent.

⇨ Now there are certain questions which often come to mind, such as:

➤ Why in spite of our willingness to improve and even after having access to such a wonderful and inspiring literature, we are still not able to achieve any significant improvement in ourselves?

➤ Why is it so, that we purchase an inspiring or insightful book from store and start reading it, however, rarely we are able to maintain the dedication with which we had started reading it and soon this half read book find its place somewhere in the bookshelf?

➤ Even if we somehow manage to read the book successfully, we seldom exhibit any improvements or change within us; apart from narrating some of the great quotes from the book to few of our friends, over a cup of coffee.

➤ Even after doing all such efforts no significant results are achieved, why is it so?

➤ Why no significant improvement or change occurs within us?

There is a common answer to the above questions and that is '**our habit of denial**'. Yes you read it right; due to this habit of ours we often fail to bring out any effective change in ourselves.

In fact, we have never ever cared to learn to develop an acceptance towards our own failures. Therefore, we not only fail in our efforts but we also fail to acknowledge those failures.

The experienced man is one who has committed many mistakes and has lived with them to an extent that now he knows what caused them, how to rectify them and most importantly how to avoid their recurrence in future.

To gain experience we need to learn, and in order to learn we need to accept our mistakes and work on them.

☛ Until we do not learn to accept and embrace our failures and losses with dignity; we cannot feel the urge to align our mind and thought process to work in unison to learn necessary skills which we might be lacking or need to develop, or work on a specific quality or a trait in our behavior or character, which might be missing or overlooked in our overall personality by us.

⇨ This newly learned skill or newly developed character trait might prove as a game changer for us.

☛ However, when we fail to acknowledge our failures, we don't evolve. Because when according to us, we have not failed at all then where is the possibility left for any self improvement?

➡ Therefore, instead of trying to learn a new skill or develop a few positive traits in our personality, we commit all of our energy and resources in blame game and finding someone else to put the blame on.

➡ This leads to an endless vicious cycle of fault finding, self pity and sympathies which further deteriorates our chances of self improvement and success.

☛ **Now let's talk in detail about the example of the half-read book, which I have mentioned earlier in the chapter:**

    ➡ Whenever we buy a book, most of the times it is because somebody close to us or someone who we consider as successful has recommended that book to us.

    ➡ We seldom buy a book because we were seeking it for the knowledge which it might contain or have keen interest in the book.

    ➡ As a result we find it very difficult to hold on to that book for long and soon it finds a permanent place in our bookshelf, with rest of the unfinished books.

It is common to fail and there is nothing wrong in failing.

Your failure signifies that you tried to do something and your willingness to accept your failure speaks about your character, level of your commitment and your sincere dedication towards your work.

Accepting to your failure not only gives you a chance for timely analysis and rectification of your fault; however, it also saves you from unnecessary explanations and time-consuming arguments, which will eventually find their way to you.

Accepting to your failure does not mean that you need to cry out loud and transform yourself into a miserable creature, and start cursing and criticizing yourself or others for failing.

However, accepting to your failure allows you to focus your energy in genuine faultfinding and seeking opinions and advices from wise. When you admit that you are at fault, you open the endless possibilities for self improvements and progress.

> There is no way to hide a mistake, if you will not accept it by today, people around you will do their best to make you accept it by tomorrow.

Acceptance is the backbone for improvement, because when we accede to anything, we configure our mind to believe in that and in turn our mind channelizes our entire potential to make it happen and as a result we exhibit change.

All that is required from us is the willingness to accept our fault and courage to get up and say these words, *"Sorry I did this and it went wrong, fault is mine and I am ready for appropriate redressal"*.

By accepting to and rectifying your mistakes, you are not only increasing your credibility but you are also increasing your confidence, experience and abilities.

Always remember that mistakes are the tools of wise, with which he sharpens his skills, enhances his experience and enriches his life.

The article was spellbinding and his words were intense, accurate, and meaningful.

It won't be an exaggeration to say that he has induced an unquenchable thirst for knowledge and enlightenment in me. He has successfully described the facts and elaborated his observations in a logically acceptable and justifiable manner.

So far, I could not find a single point or statement in his article to which I may disagree or find it hard to believe in.

To me, he appeared quite right in saying that whenever something unpleasant happens around us, it could be the negative comments given by superiors for our work or jokes played by colleagues. No matter what it is, we tend to take every remark personally and react emotionally to it.

When we are hurt, we start looking for the sympathizers and to make the situation worse the sympathies offered somehow ends up reiterating the fact that our resentment is justified and we are not at the fault.

When we have acquired so much of fake and false support for us, then instead of accepting our mistake and rectifying it, we begin exploring the world of excuses and start the process of shifting the blame on to others.

Unable to find anyone responsible for this failure of ours we put the blame on circumstances and even on the destiny for it.

We all know it is impossible to hide a mistake forever, so when we refuse to accept our mistakes that we have committed, at that very moment, we ourselves close the doors for happiness, success and prosperity in our life. Instead we subscribe to stress, heartburns, humiliation and failure.

It was really an enlightening experience. I got up from the recliner and walked downstairs, kept the notepad on the study table and walked out of the house to the lawn.

....❋ ❋ ❋..

What to do?

☞ Learn to accept the results, as they are merely the outcome of your efforts.

☞ Even if you have failed to deliver then also learn to accept your failures gracefully.

☞ Remember that you are not the first person in mankind who has failed and you will not be the last person to fail either.

☞ Committing a mistake and then accepting to it, is not a crime. However, hiding a mistake eventually leads to one. Because when you are hiding something then you start concealing, manipulating and even forging the facts, just in order to cover up your mistake.

☞ Never be afraid, because fear fails the mind and sinks the heart.

......................................❋❋❋......................................

Chapter-13

(The Thinking Notebook)

"It is beyond any debate that a positive, logic oriented and practical thinking is indispensable for leading a motivated, happy and successful life".

It was getting cold so I decided to move inside the house. When I entered the living room, I was surprised to find professor sitting on a sofa; he was busy reading a magazine.

I said as I walked towards the sofa chair placed across him, "Good evening Professor, when did you arrive?"

"Good evening dear, it's been a while" He replied while removing his reading glasses. He placed them in a cover and kept it inside his pocket. He closed the magazine and placed it on the table.

"How was your meeting" I asked after sitting on sofa chair.

Meanwhile Jerry served me with a cup of hot coffee.

Professor replied while picking up his cup of coffee from the side table, "Oh, it went well".

He started drinking his coffee.

"The articles are impeccable" I said while holding on to the cup of coffee.

Professor placed his cup back on the table and said while pointing towards the note pad lying on the study table, "I can see that, so you have read those articles. How did you find them?"

"They were amazing and helpful too." I replied with all the gratitude that I could possibly express towards him in words.

Professor said, "I am truly impressed by your dedication to learn and willingness for self improvement."

"It would be insane to lose such a remarkable opportunity to learn and improve, especially when destiny has brought you to my doorsteps." I replied humbly.

Professor smiled and took last few sips from his coffee cup before placing the cup back on the table.

I shifted a little forward in my seat and said, "Professor, the points which you have highlighted in your articles are right to an extent and now even I can easily co-relate them with the problems which I face at my work place.

You have rightly said that the solution to our problems lies within us, we just have to develop an eye to see them."

Professor shifted a little towards his right and said while taking out a big envelope from his bag and placing it on table, "I have told you many times, you are a very educated and learned man. That is why, you are able to find meaning in my words and I am sure you will be able to apply these concepts in your life."

He said while reclining a little on the sofa, "Now I can say with certainty that I have not wasted my time and energy on you, you are a student worth teaching."

(I was humbled to hear such words of appreciation coming from him. Moreover, there is nothing more enabling than acquiring knowledge and once you have it with you, then nothing appears to be insurmountable. I was feeling much more competent and capable; truly what a great feelings to have!)

After speaking these words, he paused a little and after thinking for a while, he bent a little forward while sitting on his sofa, placed his hands on his knees and said, "Son, today I will tell you about the three habits which played a significant role in shaping my destiny. These habits possess the ability to bring measureable changes in one's life, provided they are learned, practiced and implemented meticulously, in our day to day life."

He continued and said, "I have already told you about the first one, i.e. stop brooding. Now, I will tell you about the remaining two habits, which are:

1) Learn to manage your thinking process, and

2) Always analyze the situations logically."

Professor continued and said, "I will start with the first one, i.e. learn to manage your thinking process"

"Sure, sir" I replied promptly.

Professor continued and said, "The ability to manage one's thinking process is fundamental for attaining a stable state of mind. But before elaborating this concept any further, first let us talk about one of the most unique and intriguing human organ, i.e. the human brain.

The human Brain is one of the most precious and astonishing gift from the god, to the mankind.

It lies in our hands, how we make use of it.

Let us consider the following example to make our point clear and understandable:

"We all are familiar with the lenses. A single lens can be used easily to obtain different outcomes simply by changing the manner in which it is used.

A lens can be used as an eyesight correcting device in spectacles, or for taking pictures in camera or as a hand held magnifying glass to read fine prints.

The ease with which a lens can capture a far distant beautiful image with the similar ease, it can burn down things to the ashes simply by focusing the sunrays on that object.

Similar is the case with human brain, if used in positive direction with efficiency it can perform the miracles but if used otherwise, it can spell the doom."

Now, the fact which I am going to share with you clearly indicates how heavily our body spends to keep the brain healthy and running.

"Although human brain represents only 2% of the body weight, it receives 20% of the total body oxygen consumed and accounts for 25% of the total body glucose utilization".

Now consider your body as a company and the brain as a newly hired employee. Going by the hefty pay check which the company is giving to this new employee, it won't be unreasonable on behalf of the company management to expect highest levels of efficiency, productivity and professionalism from this extremely well paid employee.

Same analogy holds true for our body. Body complements the actions of brain in various ways. When brain behaves, body reciprocates even better.

When our brain is relaxed and is at peace with the surroundings, various other systems in our body also enjoy the relaxed state of functioning.

This makes us feel good, enthusiastic and energetic. Our metabolism, hormone levels and every other aspect of body is in perfect shape or we can say, is in a state of bliss.

However, when we are stressed everything inside our body, from hormones level to metabolism, from appetite to energy levels, from ageing signs to hair loss, from wrinkles on face to almost everything, just name it. Almost every system working inside our body goes haywire.

Don't forget, all of this is happening apart from the havoc that we are supposed to face on the professional grounds.

We need to understand that thinking plays a pivotal role in determining the effective and efficient utilization of our brain and consequently that of our time.

For the successful utilization of brain at its optimum levels, we need to learn to control our thinking process; and in order to do so, we need to understand the three fundamentals of thought process:

1) What to think?

2) How to think?

3) When to think?

In a way, thinking is a double edged sword. Because, to do anything properly we need to take out some time and think about it so that we can draw a plan about its proper execution.

However, more time we spend on thinking, more we feel wasted. So, we must use this facility of our brain very wisely and that too, to the best of our advantage.

Doubtlessly positive thinking is indispensable for becoming successful in life, but if overdone it can transform you into a daydreamer.

More we indulge our self in the act of over-thinking, more we lose out in terms of time available with us for implementation and the execution of the planned work.

We need to learn to treat the time spent by us on thinking at par with the money and other valuables placed by us in the bank locker.

We only take out only that much amount of money or jewelry from our bank accounts or from our locker, which is required by us to meet our requirement and after taking out the necessary amount we immediately close the locker. So that remaining amount of money stays protected.

Similarly, by constant practice we need to learn to stop the act of thinking once the point on which we want to ponder upon is addressed suitably and we have already reached at a desired conclusion and are done with the necessary planning about its successful execution.

However, the biggest problem with thinking is that it's very easy to get it started but once started, it becomes almost impossible to stop it.

☛ **Now question arises, "how to think and what to think?"**

⇨ A relaxed mind is always more efficient and productive. Therefore, before initiating any thinking process, first we should relax and try to arrive at a conflict free state of mind.

⇨ Before starting to ponder over, we must jot down some of the most relevant and important points on which we want to think. We will call these points as reference points.

⇨ These reference points will give us the framework on which lines we should start to think.

⇨ The sole purpose of establishing the framework beforehand is to help us in focusing our thinking process on the specific areas of concern rather than engaging in the act of random thinking.

⇨ The problem with random thinking is that it consumes a lot but mostly yields nothing. Although, few bright ideas might occur to you during the act but their chances of occurrence are close to rare.

⇨ However, this act of random thinking is surely going to make you an absentminded and inattentive individual. I can say this with certainty that no one prefers to have such personality especially at a work place or even at home.

⇨ On the other hand, the act of conscious thinking not only saves our time but also enables us to achieve a point at which we can convince ourselves to stop thinking further. Therefore, it's in our best interest to desist the practice of random thinking.

☞ **How to practice the conscious thinking:**

⇨ Step-I: Establishing of the reference point

➤ It must be ensured that the thinking criterion or reference points which we have selected for making our framework must be practically possible and logically feasible.

➤ Instead of some delightful and pleasing ideas, which are impossible to articulate, we should focus on something precise, achievable and reasonable to start with.

➤ We all know that brain knows no limit; therefore we need to learn to limit our thinking process, especially when it becomes necessary to do so.

By suggesting limiting our thinking process, I am not advocating to resist from creative thinking or to stop thinking out of the box. But in our day to day life or in routine businesses ventures, we don't always need an out of the box idea on regular basis.

That's why it is suggested that our first priority must be to think out appropriate solutions in a time effective manner enabling us to utilize our time and brain, most effectively and efficiently.

➡ Step-II: Piecemeal Approach:

> Break the question or the topic under consideration into smaller sections and subsections.

> Breaking complicated situations into smaller sections and sub-sections not only helps us in better understanding the situation in hand but it also helps in de-cluttering our thought process, as now we are supposed to focus on one aspect of the problem at a time.

This piecemeal approach is the key to arrive at a workable solution for very complicated problems in a time effective manner.

➡ Step-III: Make a thinking notebook:

> Once you start thinking, you must keep a notebook handy to note down whatever significant thought comes across your mind, while you are thinking on any topic, these significant thoughts can be anything, like any possible:

✓ Action plans,

✓ Precautions,

✓ Conclusions,

✓ Time estimation or any other relevant point related to time requirement of the task in hand.

✓ Or it can be any irrelevant, random or out of the box idea, which is not looking relevant at present but might be utilized later.

✓ Sometimes, these irrelevant ideas happen to help us out in dire situations.

✓ We must ensure to put down these ideas under a heading "random ideas".

✓ It is wise to maximize the use of resources and considering mind as the most potent resource which we have, it will be a pure wastage of resource to neglect even any random but useful appearing idea/ thought which comes across our mind.

This notebook will serve as a template for future planning and will help in thought reinforcement. We should name this notebook as "**thinking notebook**"

In due course of time, if you seek any modification, mention it properly in the notebook along with the reason.

Soon this book will transform itself into a blue print containing, every information from the inception of the project to its present form.

This will save your time and energy, as you are not required to rethink similar thoughts repeatedly.

Moreover, when you will sit with this notebook to think again you may come up with some newer and brighter ideas.

☞ **Now question arises; When to think?**

This is the trickiest aspect about thinking. However, I would suggest following points which must be kept in mind before initiating the process of thinking:

⇨ **Think with a relaxed mind**

➤ It is very difficult to confine the creativity by the clock or place. One can get innovative ideas in morning hours while watching sunrise or while having a bath or even over a cup of coffee or just before falling asleep.

➤ However, one thing which is worth observing here is that the most creative and effective ideas only come across our mind when we are relaxed and our mind is absolutely without any stress.

➤ It shows that brain works at its best when left at its own, that too without any external pressure or added stress.

➤ The point worth considering here is that whenever our mind is relaxed, it automatically engages itself in innovation and recreation, irrespective of space and time.

⇨ **Avoid thinking immediately after any stressful situation:**

➤ It is wise to avoid indulging in the act of thinking immediately after any heated argument/ debate or immediately after experiencing any untoward incidence; because under these circumstances our thoughts are often influenced by the ongoing emotions which invariably hinder the brain from completely conceptualizing the situation logically.

➤ When we plan to respond on the basis of thoughts which come to our mind, especially when we are emotionally vulnerable or when we have not fully conceptualized the incident or the situation in which we are; under these circumstances the solutions or plans worked out by us are often flawed.

➤ Moreover, thoughts that are generated and pondered upon in haste, often complicates the situation further instead of providing an optimum solution or redressal.

➤ Therefore, whenever you are faced with a stressful situation then instead of pouncing to ponder over it immediately, just take a five and comeback.

➤ If possible, avoid thinking about the incidence even after that short break because mind also need a little time to get rid of the rebellious emotions like anger, hatred or fear. Moreover, what is done is done; we can't undo it, no matter how hard we keep thinking about it. Therefore, it is always advisable to think with a fresh mind.

⇨ **Learn to stay calm and focused:**

➤ Instead of immediately reacting to any untoward incidence in haste; relax and try to focus on the work which you were doing prior to the occurrence of that incidence.

➤ Learn to pretend as if nothing has happened.

➤ By a little practice, you will be able to achieve the balanced state of mind which will enable you to act and respond as per your own wish and not merely as a spontaneous response to any external stimulus.

➤ When you are finally able to resist the temptation for reacting and giving an instantaneous response to any unpleasant event or incidence, you will be able to enjoy two distinct advantages over rest of the people around you and these are:

> 1) You will be considered as one of the most centered, poised and a matured employee, who knows how to carry himself. Hence, you will be considered more dependable and efficient.

> 2) Secondly, you will be able to provide yourself with an ample amount of time necessary to analyze and properly understand the situation before responding, thereby minimizing any possibility of error in your judgment and further reducing your chances of missing out on any important facts or point which you might have used in your counter but was not able to use it due to haste.

⇨ **De-stress yourself:**

➤ By now, we already know that the best thoughts and ideas come across our mind when it is relaxed; therefore, there is absolutely no point is wasting our time and energy on thinking, especially when we are stressed.

➤ Instead, just take out some time from your schedule and do whatever it is possible for you to de-stress yourself.

➤ To sum up, it is always advisable to think when you can think straight, as this will yield good workable solutions and above all it saves us a lot of time and energy.

⇨ Always remember that before implementing any project or task, make sure that you are already done with all the thinking, planning and 'what might go wrong analysis' part of the project which you are about to begin with.

⇨ This will not only boost up your confidence and efficiency but will also improve the quality of your decision making, because now your mind is no longer engaged in any last minute planning, but is free to observe and analyze the what and how of the process or the work under execution.

⇨ With your 'thinking note book' on your side, you will be able to appreciate the significant difference in the manner in which you will be able to handle your day to day affairs at work and any deviations from the normal course.

⇨ By now, it is clear that the thinking process possesses an innate potential to shape the human brain.

➤ It can carve out an achiever out of you or can transform you into a daydreamer.

➤ It can make you the expert at work or transform you into a baffled man with no plans at all.

Therefore, we need to learn to control our thinking process, in order to harness the extensive brainpower which god has bestowed on us.

It is beyond any debate that a positive, logic oriented and practical thinking is indispensable for leading a motivated, happy and successful life.

Professor said while shifting a little in his chair, "That's all about how to manage your thinking process"

"Now, I will talk about the second but one of the game changing qualities that we all need to appreciate and learn" He said, as he stretched his hand to pick up a glass of water placed on the centre table.

His content was so informative and narration so vivid and convincing that I was not willing to interrupt his flow of thoughts with any question. So, I silently kept listening to him.

After having the glass of water he started with the next topic

✳ ✳ ✳

What to do?

Make a thinking notebook with following format;

Date	Topic/ fact / situation under consideration	Possible ideas/ thoughts that came to mind	The applicability and implications of the idea or the thought

We need to dedicate few pages of this thinking notebook for jotting down random ideas that might occur to us while focusing on something specific.

Date	Random Idea	Its implications	Situation or incidence when we can use it

Chapter-14

(Logical Analysis of a Situation)

"Logic helps us thinking rationally"

Professor continued and said, "first we need to understand the meaning of the terms 'logical analysis' and 'logic' before we may start exploring this topic any further.

Broadly speaking, logical analysis is the comprehensive study of the available arguments with the sole purpose of thoroughly understanding the situation in hand, in order to arrive at a suitable conclusion.

Whereas logic helps us to understand what has actually happened, why it happened and what went wrong?

⇨ It won't be completely out of the line to accept to the fact that it's our logic which enables us to differentiate between the truth and a narrative; between a fact and the fiction.

⇨ Logic serves as a reference point to check the correctness of our perceptions, thoughts and subsequent decisions.

⇨ Above all, logic helps us in thinking rationally, especially when our emotions are doing their best to influence our judgment.

⇨ A person well acquainted with the logic is better able to appreciate the importance of critical-thinking in life."

I was having a fair idea about logic but was completely unfamiliar to the concepts of logical analysis and critical-thinking. Quite big terms! Isn't?

Frankly speaking, the today's monologue was becoming a little too much for me to assimilate at once. My confusion was very much evident on my face.

Sensing my confusion professor said (while explaining this new concept to me), "Critical thinking is one's ability and willingness to evaluate one's thoughts and thought process without any prejudice."

He continued and said, "When we open up ourselves to embrace the concept of critical thinking in our life, we start developing an increasing acceptance towards the logic and gradually we learn to over-ride the emotional barriers which often withhold us from taking the just decisions which are essential for becoming successful in life.

Eventually, we start unlocking, harnessing and realizing the immense brain power which is often left suppressed and under-utilized mainly due to following reasons:

> Our own ignorant and entangled thoughts,

> Illogical explanations and biased approach,

> Tendency of having negative perceptions

> Our reluctance to move out of our comfort zone

Have you ever realized that we spend a large portion of our life in giving away illogical, unjustifiable and hypothetical explanations for the mess in which we are?

The sole purpose of all these explanations is simply to justify our tendency of denial to move out of our comfort zone.

Most of us have got a completely normal life, but we complicate it. Yes, you heard it right; we complicate our lives with our own prejudiced decisions, unwillingness to leave our comfort zone and aching egos.

We keep on forcing our mind to accept this fabricated junk that we are facing the hardship in life without any justifiable reason and that too without any fault of ours.

This is done solely to hide our failures in correcting our priorities and our inability in modifying our unhealthy habits.

Simply in order to escape the accountability of the untoward events which are happening in our life, we never even try to analyze anything based on logic and facts.

On the contrary, we put in our best possible efforts to destroy all the rationality that might be left in us.

Gradually our subconscious mind starts accepting these false and debilitating narratives and negative auto suggestions.

Consequently, instead of devising and executing a coping mechanism to sort out the problems in which we are; our mind starts accepting that we don't have left with any control or say in the prevalent circumstances.

As a result, our mind accepts the defeat and start showing the signs of distress and malfunction, which are often exhibited in our behavior as:

- ➢ Confusion in thoughts, which subsequently starts exhibiting in our actions,
- ➢ Timorous nature,
- ➢ Low self esteem,
- ➢ Short temperedness,
- ➢ Unwilling to accept responsibility,
- ➢ Finding it difficult to socialize and to maintain the existing relationships.

Problems don't end here; unfortunately all of above characteristics further complicate our already miserable situation, making it very difficult for us to come out of this vicious cycle which keeps on going uninterruptedly.

We need to understand that, the way in which we think and the manner in which we analyze the situations have a long term effects on our

- ➢ Personal life,
- ➢ Professional life,

- ➢ Social life, and
- ➢ Mental and physical health

A person having logical thinking has got more positive approach while dealing with the challenging situations, mainly because he is able to trace the problem to its root cause.

In case, if he is not in a position to solve the problem in hand then also he always have a valid reason behind his inability in doing so and if provided with the appropriate facilities and favorable conditions he will try his best to resolve the situation as early as possible.

Even if he is not able to resolve his problems, he still have got his peace of mind because he knows that he has not left any stone unturned to sort out the issue.

When you know that you can't do much about the circumstances then you simply move on with your life to explore new horizons.

Thinking logically not only helps us in understanding the situation better, but it also helps us in eliminating the most damaging trait from our mind, that is the '**Fear of unknown**'.

When we try to understand the logic behind any incidence or event then eventually we are able to understand what is behind our loss.

This information is not only enlightening but proper understanding of the situation spares us of further self-inflicted degradation and therefore, we are able to stop blaming our losses on our;

> - Bad luck,
> - Destiny,
> - Lack of Resources and
> - All other possible expressions of self pity.

Usually we hold everyone and almost everything around us (apart from ourselves) responsible for our failure.

Whereas, it's the Logic which provides us with concrete reasons and exact cause of our failure rather than a vague idea of what might have gone wrong."

He paused for having a glass of water and then continued with his monologue, "Now I will talk about another important aspect of problem solving and that is – Analysis. Analysis is the tracing of the things to their source.

If you can somehow, manage to keep your emotions out of play and try to answer the following:

> - What went wrong?

> - When it went wrong?

➢ Why it went wrong?

Simply by finding answers to the above golden triad most of the situation can be resolved. Further, you will be also able to appreciate this basic fact that problems speak for themselves and that too in volumes; we just have to condition ourselves to listen to them.

☛ **What do we get by doing logical analysis of the situation?**

⇨ Logical analysis of a situation gives us:

➢ Solution instead of an excuse,

➢ Reasons instead of criticism,

➢ New plans for future instead of brooding over the past,

➢ Makes us more aware and alert instead of depressed, and

➢ Provide us with an opportunity for introspection, instead of the indulging in the ritual of self pity.

➢ It makes us more reliable, dependable and optimistic about life and possibilities which ultimately leads to an improved quality of life.

☞ **Now question arises, how to do the logical analysis of a situation**?

It's a multistep process, and like any other important technique we need a relaxed state of mind to begin with.

Therefore, the first step is to relax

⇨ **Step-1: 'Calm down and take a deep breath'** (can follow any relaxation technique that works for you)

⇨ **Step–2: 'Evaluate the situation like a neutral party'**:- Find the elaborated, comprehensive and apt answers for the questions of 'Golden Triad'

⇨ **Step-3: Make a chart clearly defining the every step of the process from the beginning;**
Provide necessary details against each step, details like:
> The work which was done,
> Methods used for getting the work done,
> The result obtained.

⇨ **Step-4: Now write down a neutral report for each step**; pointing out every possible short coming that was observed in

> Planning,

> Management,
> Execution,
> Resources.

➡ Step – 5: After doing a comprehensive review, draw a final inference about

> What went wrong?

> Why it went wrong?

> When it went wrong? And

> How to rectify it?

➡ Step – 6: Now read out your report to yourself; and compare it with what you have done in past.

These efforts will not only give you a clear picture of what is needed to be done but also the process and the results obtained in due course will also make you a lot wiser, experienced and a balanced person in general.

With these words he concluded his lecture.

He smiled at me and said while opening the packet that he had placed on the table, "Here is the outcome of my research which I was doing from quite some time and this is what brought me to your doorstep".

It was a book, titled, 'The uninvited guest who changed my life- 11 traits of motivated living and clear thinking'

He said while handing over the book to me, "Son, I really had a great time while staying here with you and working on this project of mine. I am deeply touched by your benevolence and an undiminishing will to learn. Please accept this copy as a token of my appreciation for your support and company."

I quickly got up from my seat and said while humbly accepting the book from him, "Thank you professor, I will surely read this one and in fact I am sure that this book is going to become my reference book for all future troubles."

He smiled, gently patted on my shoulder and left for his room, whereas I remained seated on my chair, thinking how much I have gained in these days. Almost everything around me has now transformed.

I thanked my friend for paying back unknowingly for whatever good I might have done to him in past. Now I can say with certainty, that day, God converted my thoughts into reality only to help me.

Next morning the professor left for his home, leaving behind a life time experience for me and the teachings which were to cling for long.

✳ ✳ ✳